Unclaimed Baggage

To Sharon.
Blessings to
you.

Susan McCulloh
Marcee Corn

Unclaimed Baggage

MARCEE CORN *AND* SUSAN MCCULLOCH

Archway Publishing books may be ordered through booksellers or by contacting:

Archway Publishing
1663 Liberty Drive
Bloomington, IN 47403
www.archwaypublishing.com
1-(888)-242-5904

ISBN: 978-1-4808-0352-7 (sc)
ISBN: 978-1-4808-0353-4 (e)

Library of Congress Control Number: 2013919877

Printed in the United States of America

Archway Publishing rev. date: 11/20/2013

Contents

Prologue

JAMES: JULY 14, 1925

Edith flies through the hospital doors, slamming them against the brick wall with no regard for them. The crash resonates throughout the hospital waiting room, and all eyes focus on my anxious wife demanding their momentary attention. I trail behind her, trying to keep up, clutching the small hands of our two little girls. Edith knows the familiar routine. After all, she has done this twice before.

Following my wife, we approach a long Formica-topped counter. I kneel on the floor as Edith proceeds to make a scene for all to hear. I look deep into Shirley and Glory Ann's eyes and try to explain to them, in the best way I can to their childish understanding, what is about to happen. After my explanation, I walk the girls over to a row of vacant chairs in the waiting room.

I place each of them in a straight-backed wooden chair as I look down the row of seats lining the wall of the stark white room holding others that also wait patiently for a new chapter of their lives to begin. I kiss each of my daughters gently on the cheek and return to Edith's side.

Without a word to our girls, Edith waddles in her normal fast pace, clutching her overextended belly, already focusing on the task at hand. I watch her as we go, searching for the familiar words that will be etched on the glass windowpane of the door telling her where to go. A white-clad nurse, suddenly surprised at all the commotion down the hall, sees Edith barreling toward her. I watch her brace as my pregnant wife pushes past her through the delivery room door. As the young woman is almost knocked off her feet, her cheery smile is quickly replaced with a look of utter dismay. The young nurse's white, rubber-soled shoes squeak loudly on the freshly polished tile floor as she suddenly moves. Her inexperience is quickly masked when she composes herself while straightening her pointed cap and adjusting the seam of her white stockinged legs.

I am distracted from the scene as Edith rushes across the opened room and climbs up onto the gurney before I can assist her. I sheepishly smile at the astonished young nurse and try to apologize for Edith and her determined behavior. It seems I spend most of my days doing that. Suddenly Edith grabs the sides of the rolling bed and tightly shuts her eyes. I can almost feel the pain pulsating through her belly. She refuses to utter a sound, which doesn't surprise me.

Trying to help in some way, I take a freshly wetted towel that the nurse hands me and place it on Edith's brow. Not a word is exchanged between us. Momentarily, the old doctor enters the small, muggy room clasping his clipboard in his sweat-drenched hand. He does not speak to me or Edith, but gives a simple nod in my direction. He then methodically begins to prepare for our baby's arrival. I realize then that it won't be long now before I can meet my new child as Edith heaves her body forward, trying to sit up to ease her recurring pain.

An old fan above our heads, caked with years of dust, circulates much too slow to cool us on this hot July afternoon. As the nurse blots the sweat from the doctor's brow, he pushes his sliding gold-rimmed glasses higher on his nose and takes a seat on the well-positioned stool at the foot of the gurney, readying himself for the delivery. With this action, he glances in my direction once again, and I know it is time for me to leave. I kiss Edith gently on the forehead and take my leave to join my daughters in the waiting room, allowing the doctor and Edith to complete the task before them. Slowly I make my way down the long corridor, and as I am about to open the doors at the end of the hall, I hear the loud cry of a child. At that moment, without any fanfare or excitement, I know that my baby is here. A tear wells in my eye as I push open the doors to see my daughters waiting where I have left them.

Within what seems like a very short time, the cheery nurse comes through the double door and approaches me as I wait. I study her smiling face as she says, "Congratulations, you are a father of a beautiful baby girl."

My two daughters jump from their chairs and clap, happy that they have a new sister. I smile and follow the nurse to Edith, where I find her sleeping. The nurse then asks if I want to come to the nursery to see my daughter. Since Edith is resting, I whisper, "Yes."

We walk slowly to the nursery window farther down the hall. Peering through the thick glass, I search for my child. I press my face against the glass, hoping to get a better look, and immediately recognize my own. I realize then that I can't hold back the tears that are uncontrollably streaming down my face. I watch as the nurse picks up my baby girl and carries her over to the door. I run to that place and open the door. With the light from a single bulb hanging above my head, I take the child from her and admire her delicate face, the beautiful details there. Her dark brown eyes are wide open, and she looks at me without uttering a sound. I can't keep a smile from enveloping my face as I look lovingly at this quiet, wide-eyed beauty cradled in my arms. I know at this moment that my love for this child is unconditional, as I feel the love flow between us, creating a special bond between father and daughter.

On July 14, 1925, God lovingly gave His gift. He created this little girl in His own likeness. He filled her with kindness, humor, creativity, meekness, and joy. He bestowed upon her a gift for music and art. He saw that she was good, very good. Her name was Martha.

CHAPTER 1

LAKESIDE: AUGUST 2005

"ALZHEIMER'S" LEAPED OFF THE NEATLY PAINTED sign as if in neon, beckoning the driver to come on in. Unmindful of her surroundings, Martha happily chatted away about her day as the other occupants of the car rode in a dread-filled silence. They slowly approached the portico door. The only other sound heard was the steady crunching of the gravel as the tires slowly rolled to a stop. Martha was completely content to be spending the day with her three daughters.

Marcee was the first to exit the car. Though Martha wasn't aware of it, Marcee had exited ahead of the little group to secretly release the lock on the double doors that was keeping all the residents safely inside. Once everyone had gotten out of the car, they all proceeded to the light-filled lobby. As the three sisters searched for the gentleman they came there to see, Martha was distracted by the colorful yellow-headed parrot caged in the corner. Her thoughts began to drift...

BUSCH GARDENS: JUNE 1968

The colorful parrot perched on Bob's shoulder ever so slowly turns its head to look at him. It tilts its head to the side and slowly, very slowly, starts to lower its head and open its pointy, black curved beak. Its beautiful yellow head angles to one side as if in slow motion. Bob pleads with Leslie to look at the camera, but she is pouting and tired and doesn't want to participate. I know Bob is trying to be patient with her, but it is hard for him. The parrot continues to reach ever so slowly with its mouth opened toward Bob's collar.

With its beady eyes, the parrot looks and slants his head once more toward Bob's eyes. Bob doesn't notice, but I do. Suddenly, that sly parrot reaches with his opened razor-sharp beak, grabs Bob's tiny collar button, and jerks it off faster than I can shout. In an instant, Bob slaps at the colorful parrot, and it flies off with feathers flying and mouth squawking. All three girls start laughing very hard, and that is when I take the shot. It was perfect. No one was posing, no one was ready, and it was the best photograph of the whole trip...

I know this parrot ... Martha thought. *He's in Busch Gardens. He just pecked the button off Bob's collar, and I got a great picture of it.*

She smiled but then became confused. *Is that where I am ... Busch Gardens, Florida?*

Just then, the gentleman they were to meet, Gordon, stepped out of his window-walled office with an outstretched hand to welcome the ladies. Turning to Martha, he embraced her and pecked her on the cheek as if he had known her for years. Forgetting the parrot, Martha cheerily chimed, "Hi, Doctor!" with seeming recognition.

Gordon glanced at his watch and, seeing that it was eleven o'clock, said, "Please excuse me for a just a moment, ladies." He waltzed across the room for his unofficial daily appointment. The ladies all watched and listened. He slowly walked over to an elderly, uniformed gentleman sitting in the corner by the front doors.

"Hi, Harry. Are you waiting for the bus?" Gordon said.

"Yes," Harry replied, "I believe it is a little late today."

"Well …" said Gordon, repeating these words as he does every day, "PanAm just called and said that your flight was cancelled for today. Wouldn't you know … you get all dressed in your uniform and then it gets cancelled?"

Harry looked disappointed.

Gordon chided him with loud and friendly laughter. "At least you hadn't gotten all the way to the airport this morning!" He added, "I guess it was a good thing the bus was running a little late today." "Yep," Harry replied, "tomorrow is another day!" With that, Harry got up, his hat in his hand, and headed toward the elevator doors.

As Gordon headed back over to his new charge Martha, he knew this scene with Harry would play out at the same hour again tomorrow. Gordon's questions would be the same, and Harry's responses would be just as scripted. To Gordon, however, nothing about his daily encounter with Harry was routine. It was so much more. Those special interactions were the reason Gordon had chosen to become the Director of the Lakeside Alzheimer's Assisted Living Facility.

"Follow my lead," Gordon had directed yesterday when the sisters visited to fill out the paperwork for their mother, Martha. These words were planted in their thoughts as he approached them again.

Taking Martha by the arm, Gordon whisked her off into the dining room with the sisters trailing behind like lost puppies following their master. He seated everyone at the table saying that they would be his guests for lunch. Martha was surprised that the doctor has asked her group to have lunch with him, but enjoyed her meal nonetheless. In fact, she spent lunch chatting loudly with the ladies at the next table completely unaware of the events about to unfold. The rest of the group, however, were very subdued knowing that they were about to leave their mother in this facility for the rest of her life.

Upon finishing lunch, Gordon asked Martha to walk with him as the three sisters followed behind. The two of them chatted together while walking through the hallway. Before long, they reached Martha's room. The door to her new home had a newly positioned name on it, announcing her arrival. Gordon stopped at the sign and asked Martha to read the name. "Martha!" she exclaimed. "That's me." As her voice rose, her daughters' hearts sank.

Martha disappeared with her caregiver into the music room while the daughters stole away with heavy hearts and broken spirits. They didn't know it at the time, but God's perfect plan was slowly unfolding before them.

CHAPTER 2

SPRING 2005

THE DAUGHTERS STILL QUESTIONED WHETHER the decision to leave their mother under the care of complete strangers was the best one. While the women were distraught about leaving their mother, each knew in their heart they had made the right decision. As confusion had begun to take over parts of Martha's mind, each sister had had a unique experience with her. Each experience was different, but each one resulted in the same conclusion. The sisters could not care for their mother any longer. They could not provide what she needed and wanted. And, most importantly, they each felt they couldn't make her happy.

LESLIE: SPRING 2005

The family was anxiously awaiting our arrival. My husband, Bob, was happy to see Mom and welcomed her into our home. Upon stepping inside the front door, Mom noticed him as if for the first time. Suddenly a look of utter shock and distaste appeared on her face. I hadn't seen this look before, and it was disconcerting. Mom had always loved Bob and was always happy to see him.

Doing my best to brush aside the worry, I handed Mom's suitcase to Bob to carry to the guest room. Mom saw the children and even hugged them, but as they spoke to her, she was distant and their names and faces seemed to elude her. As Bob appeared in the room again, Mom's angry gaze settled on him once again. He stepped forward to give her a long hug, but Mom clearly didn't want to hug him. Instead, she backed up against the wall as he approached. His arms still embraced her, but the embrace was not returned. She even shook herself free of his hold and brushed her arms off as if to wipe any unwanted feelings away.

As Bob turned away, he heard Mom telling me that I'm "living in sin" with this man and that we should be ashamed to have had four illegitimate children together. Bob turned again to listen more closely to the conversation. This caused Mom to wheel around to tell him that she was discussing something private with her daughter and that it was none of his business!

At this point, I realized that something was very wrong with her. She seemed confused and did not seem to know anyone in the room but me. I sat her down and explained to her that Bob and I had been married for twenty years and that we had four children. Mom was not convinced. She got mad again and stormed off to her room, slamming her door on the way. She truly believed that I was living with my boyfriend and our four illegitimate children, none of whom she knew.

The visit, which was mom's last, remained stressful and uncomfortable and no one was able to convince her of the truth for the entire two weeks. Mom was very unhappy.

SUSAN: SPRING 2005

When I arrived home with Mom for an extended visit, my husband Francis was cleaning the pool in our backyard. He always looked forward to mom's visits. He had always felt like he had a special place in her heart since he was in the Navy and mom loved the Navy. Francis's last minute job was to clean our pool so it would look nice when she arrived. As Mom went out from the kitchen door to the patio, she nodded to Francis. He stopped what he was doing to go over and hug her.

As he approached, Mom thanked him for making the pool so clean and inviting. Without stopping for her usual hug, she walked past Francis over to the lounge chair in the corner of the pool's patio and stretched out as if to enjoy a day in the sun. He tried approaching her again. She squinted and shielded her eyes from the sun as he approached. She then asked him to get her some cold lemonade from the kitchen. Francis smiled and told her that he was glad she was there and headed to the kitchen where I was preparing lunch for the three of us.

I had seen the interchange with Francis and Mom and had to admit it was really odd to see Mom stretched out, face turned towards the sun with her blue jeans hiked up to her thighs, as if trying to get a suntan. Francis told me that Mom had asked for some cold lemonade. I told him that we didn't have any lemonade and gave him a Diet Pepsi to take to her instead. With that, he proceeded to the pool with the Diet Pepsi in hand.

As he approached mom, he noticed her digging in her pocket.

She looked up and smiled at him and said, "Thank you young man, now how much do I owe you? Or can I put it on my tab?" Then, she took a sip of her drink and yelled, "This is NOT lemonade!"

Francis quickly answered by saying in a much quieter voice, "No, I'm sorry it isn't. We don't have any lemonade…but that is Diet Pepsi, your favorite, Martha."

Mom looked at Francis and said in a most disturbed tone, "What kind of a bed and breakfast is this? The pool boy calls the guests by their first name, serves them something they didn't order, and then brings something that HE says is their favorite! They don't even have lemonade for their guests that are out by the pool sweating to death!!" She continued, "I say again, what kind of a place is this? I want to speak to the owner, right now!"

With that, she crossed her arms across her chest. Francis realized then that mom was very confused and upset, so he came back to the kitchen where I was.

After he explained what had happened, I walked slowly out to the pool and sat in the chair next to Mom. I tried to take her hand, but she jerked it away. Instead, she proceeded to give me, the owner of this bed and breakfast, a piece of her mind. Sadness filled me as I listened to Mom recount all the reasons she was unhappy with my establishment. After several attempts to explain that she was at my home and not a bed and breakfast, I finally gave in to her crazy idea of being at a bed and breakfast. For the remainder of her visit, I was the owner and Francis was the pool boy. The icing on the cake, so to speak, that made my mind up about finding a special place for Mom came at the end of this uncomfortable and difficult last visit. I had put her on a direct flight to Birmingham, and my sister Marcee was to meet her at the gate. This scenario should not have been a difficult or a confusing one for Mom. I was sure there would be no problems. I was wrong.

MARCEE: SUMMER 2005

As the flight arrived at the gate at the Birmingham International Airport, all the passengers started to gather their belongings and walk to the front of the plane to exit. Mom apparently saw the people standing and moving but she remained seated. I guess no one thought much of an elderly woman waiting for everyone else to get off before disembarking herself. So, she remained seated and the other passengers filed past her seat.

I had gotten an escort pass in order to meet Mom at the gate. As I stood there looking eagerly for her, stranger after stranger filed past where I was standing but no Mom. The long line of arriving passengers ended. Still expecting to see my mother, I leaned forward to look down the hallway leading to the door where the plane waited. The crew emerged with their bags, closing the plane door behind them. They headed toward another gate for their next flight.

I knew Mom must still be on the plane because my sister, Susan, had put her on it. She had called me to confirm it and assured me that the flight Mom was on from Jacksonville would be on time.

I glanced at the sign above the door making sure I was at the correct gate…I was. The crew was gone, the plane door was sealed, and my mother was nowhere to be seen. I began to panic. All I could think to do was to grab one of the airport personnel and ask if all the passengers were off the plane. So, that is what I did.

I found a young woman in a United Airlines shirt standing near the counter and asked if she could please check to see that everyone had gotten off the plane that just landed from Jacksonville. The woman looked quite strangely at me for a moment, gathered her composure and then said, "Oh, I am sure they have all disembarked because the crew has already exited the plane. The crew is always last to leave the plane." Despite her obvious skepticism, I insisted that my mother must still be on the plane because I had been there waiting for her and she'd never gotten off. I glanced down the airport corridor to see if anyone looked lost or abandoned, but no one did.

My panic level was rising with each moment that passed, so I pressed the woman further. "Please, will you check the plane? I really think my mother is still on it." The woman picked up the phone at the counter and turned her back to me to call the phone on the plane.

After a long minute, she turned once again to me and said that no one was answering. "So," she answered matter-of-factly, "everyone must be off."

Not giving up, I said, "She's got to be on the plane…please, can someone go aboard and look for her?"

The woman was not used to such a request and picked up the phone to make another call.

"I will be happy to do it," I said, interrupting her call attempt.

"Oh no, that is not allowed. You are lucky you were able to come to the gate and pick your mother up with the escort ticket, you certainly cannot go onto the plane."

Given what was happening, I was especially happy that I had acquired the escort ticket! The airport was almost empty at this point, so I was relieved when the woman finally agreed that she would accompany me aboard the plane.

Impatiently, she said "I will take you onto the plane, but I am confident she's not on it and this is not in line with airport policy."

The door of the plane was now open again because the cleaning crew was arriving and loading their supplies into the door. We exchanged brief pleasantries with them and then I quickly proceeded onto the plane.

I immediately scanned to my right to look down the long aisle. There, sitting towards the back left of the plane, sat my mother looking out the little window with a pleasant look on her face.

Seeing my mother sitting there so alone and small, I ran down the skinny aisle to her row of seats and asked loudly, "Mom…are you alright? Why didn't you get off the plane?"

Mom smiled at me and whispered quietly as if not wanting to bother the other passengers, "Am I here already? I thought this was Atlanta, so I wasn't supposed to get off yet. I was waiting for the plane to take off again to Birmingham where you live."

"No, Mom," I whispered back sitting in the seat next to hers, "you are in Birmingham. Come on, let's get your things and get off now."

With those words, Mom smiled and stood to accompany me. Relieved, I thanked the attendant. She was in complete shock that the attendants had left the plane without seeing Mom there. I think she was probably a little relived that I did not make more of an issue about what had happened or insist on speaking to her boss. We exited the plane.

As I helped mother into the wheelchair I'd gotten, she began chatting about the lovely bed and breakfast she visited in Europe the week before.

The incident at the airport was only the beginning of Mom's last visit with me. I remember all too well the night when I knew it was time. It came four weeks later.

FOUR WEEKS LATER:

I was fast asleep when a creaking jolted me awake. I jerked open my eyes and there standing beside my bed stood Mom. I couldn't see the expression on her face but I knew in my gut that something was wrong.

I quickly sat up, staring at her standing in my bedroom in the middle of the night. In the darkness, I could see that she had her purse on her arm and she was dressed in her jeans and striped shirt from the day before. Her hair had been combed and then, as my eyes adjusted to the low light, I saw her face. She was smiling in a chilling kind of way. It was not the soft, small smile I had known for years. It was one of determination, accomplishment, love and absence all mixed up together in one expression.

As I asked her, "What are you doing, Mom?" she turned to go out of the room. I threw the covers off and hurriedly followed behind her.

She turned at the door and quickly walked down the darkened hall. As she made the next turn, I followed her to her destination. She was standing at the front door, turning the doorknob, trying to open it.

Again, I asked, "What are you doing?"

She turned to look at me as I turned on the hall light. She was not smiling any longer and with a determined voice said, "I am going home to Bob."

She tried again to open the door. I realized with those words that something more was going on with her. She had been confused before, it was true, and she had had trouble with her short-term memory, but she never had gotten so confused that she thought she should leave in the middle of the night with no car. And… the most disturbing part of the statement; "to Bob." Bob, her husband and my father, had been dead for three years.

As my heart sank, I turned her around to guide her to the couch. I sat next to her and told her that she couldn't go home. It was the middle of the night and it was a long way to her house. She looked at me with a distant kind of look as she argued that it was time for her to go and that Bob was calling to her.

I gave her a hug similar to the ones I used to give my children when they had woken in the middle of the night with a nightmare, but instead of the nightmare being theirs or hers, it was mine this time. I knew that the hug I gave my mother that moment was more for me than for her.

I told her that I wanted her to stay with me for a little longer. Little did I know how much more those words would mean to me in the weeks ahead.

Since it was the middle of the night, I suggested she should go back to bed and assured her we could talk about it in the morning. That seemed to satisfy her, and with a certain look of rejection and sadness, she walked with me back to my guest room.

I helped her undress and redress in her pajamas. She crawled into her bed as if she had been defeated. "Goodnight" she whispered as I turned to leave her room. "Goodnight, Mom," I whispered back.

As I lay in my bed again, listening for any sounds from her, silent tears fell from my tired eyes as I tried to imagine what had been going through her mind just a few minutes before.

MARTHA: A FEW MINUTES LATER...

I hate remembering. I hate that Marcee had reminded me. The pain of losing Bob had returned, once again filling my thoughts, and it was too much. I realize that confusion had taken over my mind, but I desperately want to return to those few moments of remembering him.

I had heard his sweet, familiar voice calling out to me. "Maaatha," he had sung out in his southern drawl. "Maaatha," he said in the voice that I so dearly loved. My one love, my beloved Bob, is gone from my life. I remember now. The familiar feeling of emptiness rushes in once again with more sadness than I feel I can bear. I close my eyes to forget. My desperate tears soak the pillow.

CHAPTER 3

BOB: SEPTEMBER 2000

I LEAVE THE DOCTOR'S OFFICE AFTER getting the diagnosis of terminal lung cancer with the words "it won't be long..." echoing in my mind. All I could think about were the things that I need to do before my death. There would be papers to file, phone numbers to be written out, people to be contacted and repairs to be done. I had to leave everything in order for Martha and the girls.

Martha and I didn't exchange many words as we drove the short distance home. Martha could only wait for me to tell her what to do.

As we reach the front door, I regain my normal strength and control. I tell my wife of fifty years to have a seat on the couch. She does as I ask. I hold her hands and tell her that I love her and that ours is a wonderful marriage. She cries as I go on.

"I want to go over my paperwork with you."

Martha looks at me with a vacant stare as she cuddles more closely. I can tell that she is not willing to comprehend what the doctor told us only an hour before. With exposed heartache painted on her face, I know at that moment that she wouldn't handle my death well.

Instead of pulling the important papers from the filing cabinet, that evening I stroke Martha's hair and let her cry into the night. After she has finally drifted off to sleep, I occupy the night searching for order in the chaos of my mind.

Wrestling with all my emotions and responsibilities, I reluctantly choose to share my thoughts with my three daughters in a letter. It will be the most important letter I will ever write.

Sitting at the desk, staring at the keyboard, and blank screen, I try to find the words for my daughters…but my thoughts return to my Martha. She would be alone now. I can hardly bear the thought of that.

I sadly question once again if I could have done more to build her confidence over the years. Could I have loved her more or, most importantly, tried harder to get her the help that she needed?

BOB, FALL 1973

As usual, the sherry bottle comes out from under the kitchen counter at about five. Martha fills her glass. I see her sipping on her favorite drink as she fixes a bowl of corn nuts and my favorite drink, planter's punch. Other nights it might be peanuts or cheese and crackers, but the routine is always the same.

When the appetizers and cocktails are ready and the evening has cooled, she calls to me to join her on our patio by the pool. We talk of our day as we enjoy each other's company and the cool ocean breezes. This part of our day is my favorite.

After an hour or so, Martha heads to the kitchen to start on dinner. She pours another sherry. As she fixes dinner, I can hear her pour yet another drink. The quality of our evening is often determined by how long it takes her to prepare dinner. She seems to do much better if the dinner doesn't take long to fix, and we eat earlier.

At the table our conversation focuses on the girls' activities for the day and what their plans are for the next few days. We are the picture of the perfect family.

Our problems begin after dinner when Martha and I retire to the den to watch our favorite television shows and the girls clean up the dishes. Since Martha has finished her sherry at dinner, she slips into the kitchen before coming to the den, filling her glass again. She assumes that I don't notice, but I always do.

At this point in the evening Martha is no longer with us. The untamed creature within has been released once again. There is little I can do.

After completing their chores, the girls come in and Martha starts picking a fight with our youngest. Some nights it is one of the other girls or me. It will be over nothing important. But whatever the topic, Martha will get mad and ugly.

This night she gets so angry that she cries and raises her voice. She ends up telling the family that no one loves her, that she doesn't deserve anyone's love, and that she has done a terrible job raising our three daughters. She will end her rant with how much she hates her life. The girls and I will try to reassure her and tell her over and over how much we love her, but it does no good. She is beyond reasoning at this point. In fact, Martha, my love, is gone. Her ugliness is in full view for all of us to see. She continues to drink and get louder and louder as she complains, slurring her words as she speaks. I ignore her. When the girls finally give up, they seek the shelter of their rooms. I try, once again, to talk to her, but there is no understanding at that point. Angry now, I too, head to our room for some peace. Ultimately, she falls asleep on the couch, bringing peace to the family once again. On some of the better nights, I can talk her into going to bed with me. The same routine happens most nights. I want so desperately to know how to love her more so that "the evil" won't emerge each evening. But alas, I remain defeated.

BOB: SEPTEMBER 2000

Shaking this reoccurring memory from my mind, I go back to the task at hand and write from my heart, to my beloved daughters:

> Dear Marcee, Susan and Leslie,
>
> Let me start by saying I love each of you so very much. As you know, I am dying. I am not ready. It is a hard concept for me to get my mind around, but the doctor says I don't have much time left now, so I feel the need to write this difficult letter.
>
> I am the head of this family, and now feel like I am abandoning the ship. The captain should never abandon the ship before the crew! As a Navy captain I find it a funny joke that God is playing on me, but in my heart I know that God has a plan.
>
> I am so sorry to be leaving you and your mother. I had hoped that God wouldn't take me first. Your mother needs me, and I am not sure how she will do without me to take care of her. I am worried about your mother. As you all know, she is not a strong woman. Therefore, I want to sit down with you to talk about all my business affairs.I am sorry I am leaving you three to these tasks.
>
> I will talk to your mother, but I need to give you my thoughts as to what she should do with the house and where she should live upon my death. I hate to burden you with all of this, but your mother will not be able to handle it. You each have your own families and it will be hard to also take care of your mother, but we have no choice here. After being married to your mother

for fifty–six years, I know she won't be able to handle the most mundane tasks of everyday life without me.

Your mother…I love her dearly. But, I need to say some words about her to you girls. First of all I worry terribly about her. As I said, she is not a strong woman. I know over the years you have witnessed your mother's undying devotion to me, sacrificing all she is for me. Love is a hard concept for her because she does not love herself. So to her, love is devotion. She loves each of you with all her heart. I know she doesn't show it always, but she does. When I was gone on deployment, she had a very hard time with life. I am sorry girls for leaving you during those times. I know that many times you had to fend for yourselves. For that I am sorry. I hope you realize that she did the best she could.

As you are well aware, your mother has very low self-esteem and she's depressed. I think it started way back with her mother and sister. Edith doted over Glory Ann and Glory Ann demanded her attention. So basically, your mother became invisible to them. Imagine living in a family where you are virtually invisible. Your mother was also devoted to Glory Ann. It was a love/hate relationship. She loved her sister for her confidence, beauty, and presence, but she hated the fact that she was not all those things her sister was.

I know you girls are very aware of your mother's excessive drinking, especially when I was gone. I think she drank to cover up the pain and loneliness she felt. I never could get her the proper help she needed. I gave her what I could. As you know I continually tried to lift her spirits by leaving her little handwritten notes declaring my love for her, but sometimes, actually most times, it still wasn't enough.

Without me here, I am not sure how your mother will do. I don't know whether she can go on living life without me. I fear she may just curl up and give up. I pray not. She will need a lot of boosting up from you three to keep her spirit going.

So in the end girls, I am sorry to be leaving before your mother. Take care of her for me, as you had to do so many times in the past while I was out to sea. Please tell her often that I love her. I want you to know that I am so blessed to have been your father. I tried to be your earthly father mimicking our heavenly Father, but find that I may have fallen short. I am so proud of the strong and independent women you have become. For that, I am so thankful. I pray for the best for you three and your mother.

I love you,
Your Dad

CHAPTER 4

LESLIE: SUMMER 2002

I WAS A MACHINE. I WAS so well trained that I knew my job forwards and backwards. I was a robot, not feeling, just doing. I worked through the notebook Dad had given me, focusing on the task at hand and not letting emotions get in the way. I had to put my family on the back burner for now. Nothing could get in the way of my promise to my Dad, nothing, not even my family.

I remember we started our sessions on a Friday. Dad had told me to leave the kids at home and to plan to come two times a week for as long as it took. The sessions were run like a business meeting. No time for niceties, and he allowed no room for confusion. He had his notebook and he had a notebook for me. I took notes, lots of notes…notes about his financial portfolio, phone numbers, the Navy, whom to write or call for what, where everything important was located, who was to get what of his and his wishes for what would happen with Mom. It was a daunting and draining task, but

I did it. I drove the two and a half hours over to their house twice a week for a year.

For a solid year I left my husband and kids and spent the night at Mom and Dad's house on Tuesday and Thursday nights so I could be there bright and early the next day for our sessions. I knew it was my duty as a daughter to do this for my Dad. He had asked me to be the executor of his will, and I was determined to do a good job. I was extremely efficient. I never let my emotions get in the way, and I never wavered or wandered from my job.

After a year, the day came when I was forced to be in charge. Dad died. My training was over, and the terrible task was at hand. We were all there when he died, but Marcee had to leave shortly afterwards to get back to work. I sent my family home. Susan and I stayed with Mom for a while longer.

I immediately went to work making calls, writing letters, and getting everything in order. I did the job that I promised my Dad I would do upon his death. I worked so hard, that every night I was exhausted by six o'clock and fell into bed. In the morning, I was driven once again to work and fulfill my promise.

Several weeks passed and it was time for Susan to leave. I knew that something was on her mind, but I didn't have any extra time to talk. My emotions had been checked at the door weeks ago. So, I avoided her and the subject of "talking" until she forced me to listen.

Mom had gone to bed early on the last night before Susan was to fly back to California. I didn't want her to go because I would be alone to deal with this job, this promise. Susan asked if I wanted to quit a little early and get into the pool with her since it was her last night. I batted her idea around in my head and finally decided that I should spend some time with her since she was leaving.

She began by talking about Mom and how she didn't think that Mom would last too long without Dad. She thought that Mom would die of a broken heart. Just as I had feared, Susan was very emotional.

We were both worried about her. We could not imagine Mom living by herself. I told Susan that I was responsible for Mom now because I agreed to take care of her and that I couldn't possibly leave Mom or go home to take care of my family. I had made a promise to Dad.

When I mentioned my own family, Susan said that there had to be a balance between my family and my mother. I did not agree. I was left with this responsibility of taking care of Mom and her affairs. I told Susan that I didn't know another way to do this job than to put my whole heart and soul into it. Plus, a promise is a promise. I loved my family, but at this point in time I felt more obligated to Mom than to my own children or husband. Susan said that I had to reach a compromise. I knew that what she said made perfect sense to most people, but it didn't to me.

I cried when Susan flew out the next morning. I knew that she had been the voice of reason for me. I knew that my own family was important, but I also knew that I had made a promise to my father and I always held tight to my promises. I knew that if Dad loved Mom enough to go through the last year of his life preparing for his death, then it was my job to carry out his wishes. I knew I would stay for as long as it took.

SUSAN: MAY 1988

I was sewing late into the night and thought to myself, *"I have to finish this last sleeve in the baby's dress before I call it a night."*

The house was quiet with all three of the girls tucked into their beds. The only sound that could be heard was from the TV in the den, as Ed McMann's familiar voice said, "Heeeeeeeer's Johnny!" Staying up until midnight and watching the Johnny Carson Show was not unusual for me while Francis was out to sea. While sewing and listening to the show, I thought, "This is my favorite part of my day." My best dog Dusty was by my side. He must have been dreaming because he was kind of growling and his feet were moving very fast as if he were running in the woods chasing after vermin. I laughed to myself and kept on sewing.

I was so proud of myself for having finished all three of the girl's dresses for the Fly-In that was scheduled in two days. Francis had been gone on deployment for seven months, and I was ready to have him home. He was stationed on the USS John F. Kennedy and flew the A-6 Bomber. Their mission during this deployment was over Lebanon.

I spent a long time picking out each pattern and the material I would to use for the dresses. I wanted each of the girls to look beautiful and feel special for when their Daddy came home. All three dresses were made out of black velvet with the same delicate white lace trim. But each dress had a unique style that was just right for each daughter. Whitney's had a dropped waist, Allie's had a natural waist and a big Peter Pan collar, and McKenzie's had an empire waist with a big bow, perfect for a two year old. I had planned well, and I was so excited to see them each in their new dress.

After finally finishing the last sleeve, I had one thing left to do. I needed to sew the tag in the neckline that said, "Lovingly handmade by Mom". While I was doing that, my mind drifted back to a time of watching my Mom sew clothes for me and my sisters.

SUSAN: NOVEMBER 1970

I remembered watching the wheel turning as Mom pumped the petal with her foot. I loved to watch Mom sew. I was totally amazed watching Mom as she took a plain square piece of material and transformed it into something beautiful. I wanted to be just like her. As I got older and ready for high school, I took Home Economics so I could learn how to sew like my Mom. Sewing came easy for me and I made most of my own clothes. I made all of my Homecoming dresses. I even made a bathing suit for myself.

I remember one very special thing that Mom had made for me when I was in high school.

For weeks before Christmas, Mom spent night after night locked up in her sewing room. She would not allow me to come in because she told me that she was sewing something very special for me for Christmas. It was rare for Mom to sew only for one of us, so that made this gift even more special to me. I was beyond excited!

As Christmas grew closer, I could hardly contain my excitement for the special handmade gift from my mother. When it was finally my turn to open a present on Christmas morning, I chose the special one from Mom first. The box was wrapped in shiny paper with a big red satin bow around it. I tore at the paper and lifted the lid on the box. Folded, inside the box, lay the most beautiful shiny, red, pleather maxi coat I had ever seen. I jumped up and ran over to my mother and hugged her as I thanked her for the Maxi coat.

She smiled and said, "You're welcome."

I ran back to my spot to finish pulling it from the box. As I raised the coat up from the box, I could see that she had lined it with red and white material. Her special tag "handmade by Martha." was sewn into the neck. "This is the best Christmas present I think I've ever gotten," I said as I continued to pull the coat from out of the box.

Suddenly disappointment overtook me. When I had pulled the coat all the way out of the box and stood to hold it up against my body, I noticed that my coat wasn't finished.

By this time, the attention had turned from me to one of my sisters as she was opening a gift. I took a deep breath and tried as hard as I could to not look disappointed. I stuffed the coat back into the box and watched as the others opened their presents.

After all the presents had been opened, Mom came over to me and explained that she did not have time to finish the coat before Christmas but she promised that she would have it finished before I went back to school after Christmas break. I wanted to believe her. She worked on it some during the next two weeks, off and on, but she didn't finish it. She never finished the coat. I never wore it, not once. My beautiful Pleather maxi coat sat on the table next to her sewing machine for years with dust settling in its folds.

Years later, after I was married, I noticed during one visit, that my pleather maxi coat was not there. It was gone from its place beside the old sewing machine. I don't know what ever happened to that coat. I never asked. But I do know that whenever I think of that coat, the same feelings of utter disappointment fill my mind and I am taken back to that Christmas morning so many years ago. Because of those feelings, I made a promise to myself. I promised that when I had children of my own and sewed for them, I would never let anything I made for them *ever* go unfinished.

SUSAN: MAY 1988

Sitting on the couch now, sipping my half-drunk glass of wine that I had poured hours before, I smile. I had finished all three of my daughter's dresses for their father's homecoming. A sense of pride and joy came over me then as I sat and watched Johnny Carson say goodnight to his audience. I reflect on how different my Mom and I are. I always thought we were similar; we both had husbands who were officers in the Navy, we both had three daughters, and we both had the good fortune to be stay-at-home moms. We both loved our families. But the similarities end there.

MARCEE: SUMMER 2002

We took great care with all the medicines we were instructed to give to our father by the hospice nurse. He hadn't been awake much lately.

"The medicines must be doing their job," I thought as I sat down for my shift. The morphine would eventually take the pain away from him forever.

As I watched my mother sleeping next to my Dad, I smiled at the sweetness of the scene. Theirs was a love story unlike any other. She was devoted to him and gathered her strength from him, and he loved her endlessly. Now he was dying, soon to be in Heaven. But what was to become of her? My sisters and I all believed the same thing; she would not be able to function or take care of herself and would likely die shortly after him, from a broken heart. Was that to be?

She had remained in the bed with him, not leaving his side, from the moment he had become bedridden. My sisters and I took care of everything for our father. She was unable.

I remember the night well. A star-studded sky hung above our heads as we sat on the dock overlooking the canal. We were exhausted and knew it wouldn't be long now. Dad's breathing was shallow, and he hadn't woken up for several days. Hospice came and went as we stayed around the clock with him. We were taking a break, just a few feet away, while Leslie's husband sat by his bed.

Susan was crying, knowing that Mom couldn't make it alone. Honestly, we all knew. Mom would be alone here at the house since none of us lived close by, and she would insist on staying in her house, with her things, remembering the way it used to be with her Bob. Leslie lived the closest so she would have the responsibility of checking in on her.

"How long do you think she will live after he is gone?" Susan asked crying.

"Not long," I said.

Leslie thought and replied with certainty, "Oh, only a few months." The conversation ended abruptly as Leslie's husband Bob called us into the bedroom. Dad passed away several hours later.

On that night, the stars shone brightly down on the sisters and

they noted their beauty and majesty. On that night, God, with his unconditional love shining down on them, His children, must have smiled because He knew that their worried minds and hurting hearts were only temporary pains. He knew what plans he had for them; plans to heal and restore them. And on that night, Martha lay next to her dying husband, afraid to face the world without him, she felt the power, love and comfort from her heavenly Father, only... she misunderstood it.

MARTHA, ON THAT SAME NIGHT...

I so love the feel of Bob's warmth against my body as I cuddle up against him. Bob gives me the strength and courage to meet my days. Just the feel of him helps me to be able to get through my day and be the wife and mother I know I should be.

When we are close like this, his strength and courage somehow rush from his body to mine giving me the power I need to fight the battles deep inside. I crave his herculean strength and count on it to combat my own weaknesses.

I know I will soon fall asleep in the comfort, security and authority of his embrace. He will never leave or forsake me.

God lovingly smiled down at his daughter as she lay there thinking those thoughts. He whispered quietly to His wide-eyed beauty, "I will never leave you nor forsake you. Trust in me for I will give you rest."

CHAPTER 5

LAKESIDE: AUGUST 2005

IF AN ENTIRE ROOM COULD be picked up lock, stock and barrel and moved to another place that would be a huge accomplishment. It was an accomplishment that Martha's daughters tried their hardest to achieve. If it were possible to make a mother feel comfortable in a place other than her home, then that was what her daughters had to do. So the three of them tried.

Before Martha was to arrive at Lakeside, Gordon had suggested that they bring up her furniture and put it in her apartment so she would feel comfortable. He suggested that they place the furniture and knick-knacks in her new room to resemble how they were placed at home.

Martha's girls went about their task doing that and more. They totally reproduced her bedroom from home, bringing every piece of furniture, every wall hanging, and every piece of bedding. They brought her bedspread and curtains from her home. Every detail was duplicated, including her "wall of family," as she lovingly called it. Anyone that meant anything in her life was there in their own frame, arranged as they had been at home.

Her dresser was at the foot of her bed and her nightstand, the same compote that sat next to her bed at home, was in the correct spot. Everything, including the throw on the antique rocking chair, was the same. Martha's daughters prayed that she would feel at home despite being hundreds of miles away.

As Gordon led her into her room that first day, he stopped by the wall of pictures to comment on her photographs of her family. He had rehearsed with the three ladies earlier in the week as to who was in each photo so he could call out each name to their mother.

As he pointed to the photo of Bob as a young ensign in the Navy, he said, "Here is a photograph of Bob in his uniform and one here of your mother and daddy." He went on discussing with Martha her entire family.

After gaining her trust, he went on to tell her that she was going to have to stay here at this hospital for a few days to get well. Dreading this part of the day and not thinking that the story would fly, the three sisters looked at each other, waiting for their mom's refusal. However, to their surprise, partly thanks to Gordon's expertise and partly because she thought he was a doctor, Martha believed his story and asked him what was wrong with her. He told her the truth, that her blood pressure was a little high and that they didn't want her leaving that day.

With those words, she looked at Susan and said, "What about Daddy? How will I let him know that I am here?"

Susan, having been put on the spot responded quickly with, "Oh… Mom, I will send a message to the Red Cross, and they will send a telegram to the ship and let him know immediately."

Martha trusted Susan's response since Susan's husband also was a naval officer, like Bob, and she trusted that Susan would know what to do.

With Susan's quick response, Martha seemed satisfied and said "Okay." The three daughters let out a sigh of relief and hoped she didn't hear it.

Their mother looked around the familiar looking room then and her only comment was, "Well, this is a nice hospital room," not recognizing any of her beloved things there.

LAKESIDE: A DAY LATER

In a room down the hall from Martha's, Harry opened his eyes as the sun shone brightly through his window awakening him. It was morning, his favorite time of the day. He hopped out of bed, opened the closet door, and pulled out his uniform, laying it across the bed.

Harry loved being a pilot. Harry loved heading to far off places in his airplane. Harry loved his job!

Harry meticulously got dressed in his PanAm Airlines uniform. He slowly buttoned every button, pulling both sides of his shirt together, noting the tightness of it, and telling himself that he must hold back the sweets for today. He slid his belt into the pant loops with a little difficulty, and neatly tucked in the starched, light blue shirt. He slipped the tie over his head, glad that he had already tied it the night before. Finally he tugged his freshly shined, tight, black shoes onto his feet and placed the captain's hat upon his head, smiling at his handsome reflection in the mirror.

Oh how women love a man in uniform he thought to himself as he picked up his keys. Getting up in the morning and slipping into his uniform was what he did every day and he loved it. It was so much more to him than a job. It was so much more than a routine to him. It was who he was.

As he closed and locked his door behind him, he saw Doris down the hall. He waved at her and she smiled at him, thinking he was such a handsome man in his uniform. As he walked past her, he nodded to her, noting that she was quite a lovely lady. Oh, how proud he was to be a pilot. "Have a good flight, Harry!" she exclaimed.

"I will Doris."

"Today is Valentine's Day," Doris yelled after him.

"Have a good day then, Doris," he sang and then whistled his favorite tune as he proceeded towards the elevator down the hall.

He traveled towards the elevator doors, passing Martha's opened door. Martha had awoken early on her second day at Lakeside and was already dressed sitting on the edge of her bed, gazing at her wall of photographs. She was especially admiring the one of Bob, in his uniform. As she was thinking about her husband, she heard whistling outside her door.

Her gaze moved from Bob's picture towards the whistling coming from down the hall. Seeing the handsome man in uniform, walking past her door, she jumped to her feet, recognizing him. It was Bob. He was home!

With excitement and a bounce to her step, she ran out her door and turned to follow the sound of the whistling, just as Harry rounded the next corner. Martha followed the happy sound.

With "Bob" not in sight, Martha soon forgot what she was doing and was quickly distracted by the smell of bacon being cooked in the kitchen.

The wonderful aroma diverted Martha's attention and she paused by the door of the dining room. Kathy, the Director of Memory Care saw the new resident and, being well aware that it is best to keep the new residents busy, she asked Martha to help her set the tables and arrange some balloons for her. Martha smiled eager to help.

The other residents slowly began to wander in for the Valentine's Day breakfast. Seeing the colorful bunch of balloons in the corner, Martha's mind slipped into a memory of long ago and lingered there...

Martha: On the Navy Base-Fall, 1970

The red, white and blue balloons grow larger and larger as the girls pump them with helium.

"What a fun party this will be!" Martha thought. The party is still a few hours away and I have so much to do. Bob had called to say that they would be pulling into the harbor in three hours. Susan and Marcee already had dozens of balloons filled.

"Everything looks wonderful." was her second thought. "Being in charge of homecoming is really difficult, but I know I have to do it. I am, after all, the Captain's wife, and I've had to lead and direct the rest of the wives often and on many different occasions. This homecoming party, like every party, has to go off without a hitch."

Getting more nervous, Martha continues to think, " It has to be perfect, with balloons, decorations, and delicious food. Most importantly, I have to look magnificent and act in a way befitting the Captain's wife. That is what Bob expects, and that is what everyone else expects of me. I love my husband and the Navy, so when I have a duty to perform as the Captain's wife, I know I can't be the timid and shy Martha that comes so much more naturally. I need to become "the Captain's wife." I need to be Glory Ann."

"As Glory Ann, I can be ready for duty."

Martha knew that over the years, it actually became easier. She made the familiar transformation several hours ago.

"It is nothing but routine now. I force my mind to drift into Glory Ann's mind for the performance." Ever since we were young, I have watched and envied my sister's grace, strength, and confidence. After so many years I can "become" Glory Ann for a few hours, imitating my beloved sister. It's a secret place that only I know about and where only I can go. My older sister, Glory Ann, is confident, beautiful, and can capture a room with her smile. As Glory Ann, I can do anything. I can be confident and in control.

The younger women always look up to and listen to me since I have the most experience as a Navy wife. Not only do I run the social functions for the ship, I teach these younger women the way things go in the Navy. It's my job to remind the women of their roles as Navy wives and set the standard for how they should act in these situations. This "Welcome Home" party will be, like all the other parties; wonderful and welcoming for the men returning home. It will be perfect and Bob will be so happy.

LAKESIDE: FEBRUARY 2006

Martha's heart starts to race as she realizes that the "Welcome Home" party is going to begin very soon and nothing has been done. It is her responsibility to decorate and have everything ready. The balloons for the party dangle from the ceiling in the corner of the room and Martha is beginning to panic. She has to get these ladies moving and working because the men will be home soon and there is a lot to do. Her anger begins to surface. She notices the phone in the corner of the room then. *Why isn't Bob calling?* He always calls when they are two to three hours out so Martha can have everything ready when they arrive in port. The phone is not ringing to tell Martha where Bob is. She stares again at the tan colored phone on the table. *Where was he?* She has a party to get ready for. The wives are here, and there is no time to waste.

"Go get those balloons!" she barks at the nearest woman pointing to the pink, red and white balloons in the corner. The older woman stares at Martha not knowing what to say.

Martha immediately spins on her heel and barks at another woman, "Set the table, please!"

The other woman looks bewildered and simply says "No," and does not move.

Martha is not used to the women not following her orders to the letter. She grows angry.

Shouting loudly she screams, "We have to set the tables, now!" and runs to the nearby kitchen to gather the paper plates, forks, cups and napkins.

Hearing all the commotion from the dining room, Kathy steps out of the kitchen and stops Martha. With her arm gently around Martha's shoulders, Kathy guides her out of the doorway of the kitchen where she stands, and into the Gathering Room.

"What are you so upset about, Martha?" she pleads gently.

"Well…the party is in a few hours and we have to get ready, where is the food and the cake? I just can't have this on my watch!" Martha wails. She starts to cry as she speaks. The ship, Bob and all the other men aboard will be here soon, and we are NOT ready!"

"It will be O.K. Martha," Kathy whispers as she pats her arm. Changing the subject quickly, Kathy exclaims, "Oh, I forgot to tell you, Bob called."

Martha's frown transforms quickly into huge smile as she glances at the tan phone in the corner of the room. Between the tears, she asks "What did he say? Where is he?"

"Well," Kathy lingers, thinking ahead quickly while she speaks, "He wanted me to tell you that he has been delayed. He is still on the ship, but it won't be coming in today. It'll be arriving later." Kathy holds her breath as she waits for Martha's delayed response.

Finally Martha quietly says, "Well, that happens sometimes, we have to be flexible here. Sometimes the ship gets delayed. I have had to deal with this before. We will simply delay this party until they come in."

With that she stands, turns toward the dining room and shouts to the women standing around, "Ladies, attention please, I have just gotten word that our men will not be in today. Don't worry. They are simply delayed. It happens all the time in the Navy. We will have our party on the day they arrive."

The other women listen to Martha and Doris even says, "Oh, goody, a party! I like parties. Are men coming?"

Kathy shakes her head as she chuckles. Another meltdown is averted and for that she is glad. That old, tan phone that sits disconnected in the corner has come in very handy and has been a wonderful prop to have over the few months that I have worked upstairs in the Memory Care Unit. She had learned as much as she could about each of the resident's past and had become a very creative thinker and comforter. She even brushed up on her skills as an actress, which she found had been the most important talent she could pull out of her bag of tricks. Each of her beloved residents had remembered from time to time scenarios from their past and as if in a play, often times acted them out. She is thankful for the little bit of drama training she had in the past and that she seems to be pretty good at it.

CHAPTER 6

LAKESIDE: JULY 2006

MARTHA BELIEVED THAT BOB was alive again. Gordon had explained to her children during a meeting with him earlier. "Don't argue with your mother about what reality is," he said gently. "She only knows what she thinks she knows. If you try to convince her of the truth, she will get upset and won't understand. So, just agree with her".

As the days went on, and as her daughters would come to visit her, she would always say, "Oh you just missed your Father. He must be in the other room." Other times she would say, "He is gone today." She always thought Bob was out flying or fishing or, more often than not, "out to sea."

Her girls always would say, remembering Gordon's advice, "Oh I am so sorry I missed him! Maybe I will see him later," or some such reassurance. As difficult as it was for them to talk of their father as if he were still alive, Gordon had been right, but they had to learn it the hard way.

It was exhausting to live through such difficult situations. In a moment of selfishness, one of them would try to explain to her that Bob had died four years before and that he wasn't there.

Immediately, as the memory of that time was recalled once again in Martha's mind, all the sadness, loneliness, and depression filled her mind. Her tears and the look of utter devastation on her face were gut-wrenching for her daughters.

They knew at that moment that none of them would ever bring his death up again. Thankfully, after a few minutes, it was soon forgotten once again as they distracted her with an activity with some of the other ladies. Martha thought Bob was there with her, and her daughters loved her too much to take that away from her. She was reliving her times with him. She was happy, so happy.

Martha lived, once again, with her beloved Bob. He never came home, of course, but each day was new to her, and each day brought the excitement of her love's return.

MARTHA: NOVEMBER 1943

I am awakened this morning to the sun streaming onto my face from the large window next to my little bed. Even though it is cold outside, the heat baths my face and surges somehow into my heart. I want to linger a few minutes more in its glow before putting my feet on the cold wooden floor. My mind drifts off to last evening.

I had officially met Bobby. Oh, I had noticed him before on the occasions when I had briefly seen him in the apartment waiting on the other girls. Glory Ann had even asked me once if I wanted to go with them all to a club. I was not really interested in the New York City night life so I refused. I had never even made eye contact with Bobby, but last night, for the first time, he spoke to me. He sought me out, and we spoke for a few minutes. He had been nice and that had surprised me a bit. He had not seemed like the kind of boy that would be nice to me. He was so sure of himself, so confident, so handsome, and so popular. All of Glory Ann's roommates and Glo herself seemed to vie for his attention. But last night, he seemed to want to talk just to me. I hope I hadn't just dreamt it now that morning is here.

Things just did not usually happen this way to me. When Glory Ann and I are in the same room, everyone wants to talk and to be with her. After all, Glory Ann is outgoing, beautiful and full of life. No one ever chooses to speak to me if she is there. After all, I am quiet and uncomfortable, and with my tiny frame I know I simply fade into the wallpaper. That is the way it is and would always be.

This morning as I think again about the night before, I grow more confident that I had not read him correctly. I must have misunderstood his intensions. It is silly to think otherwise.

I lie here feeling a small bit of warmth deep in my heart, a feeling I am unaccustomed to. I think then of his face, his eyes in particular. He has piercing grey eyes that had looked, really looked deep into mine. They drew me into him from the first look, pulling at me with a magnetism there that was impossible to refuse. They had the appearance of hard, cold steel but, deceivingly, they weren't hard and cold at all, but rather molten and warm as if they were melting my heart and inviting me in. Last night, his look pierced into my soul, reading everything that was written there. That had made me uncomfortable, so uncomfortable in fact, that I had had to shift my gaze to the wall behind him in order to avoid the feeling of embarrassment and shyness that had overwhelmed me. I was not used to feeling so vulnerable with a complete stranger, or with anyone for that matter.

Then my thoughts shift to his lips. They are big and smiling and talking all at the same time. Trying to remember what we had talked about, I can only picture them moving and can't remember the words that came from them. Laughing, I think that they look kind of spread out all over his face. The ends of his mouth are turned up slightly giving him a mischievous look.

His brown hair is very short but the texture seems thick like his eyebrows.

He has a wonderful scent of sweat and sweet and man all rolled into one, but his voice is what drew me in the most.

He also has a very southern drawl that I am not accustomed to. I found it very difficult to understand him at times. I love the way he says my name. He simply draws out the "a" for a long moment, making my name sound special and different and actually beautiful.

"Maaaaaatha," I whisper to myself mimicking his voice. I am surprised at the sound of my own voice and look around the room quickly to make sure no one hears me.

As I look around, I see that the room is empty and the door closed. My two roommates must have already gone to work. I glance at my clock on the dresser then and realize that I had stayed in bed too long.

Shaking the thoughts from my head, I jump from my little bed to my slippers and grab my bathrobe from the end of the bed. It is cold and I want to hurry to get into the hot shower to warm up. I skirt around the crowded bedroom to the door and open it to find Glory Ann standing in the kitchen. She is drinking a glass of tomato juice and turns to smile at me. I smile back and make a beeline for the bathroom.

Once inside, I close the door tightly. *She knows!* Somehow Glory Ann knows that Bobby and I had had a moment last night, a moment that I can't shake from my head. *Why does Glory Ann have to be a part of everything?* I tear off my robe and pajamas and hop into the shower as the hot water steams over me. I stand for a long time trying to let the warm water rinse away the memory and the longing from my heart.

I know Glory Ann is waiting for me as I shower. When I can't put off the inevitable any longer, I open the bathroom door and see my big sister sitting on my bed.

"What are you doing?" I ask her.

"Well young lady….did you think you would slip out of here this morning without telling me about what happened last night? Hmm?"

"Oh nothing happened last night. What do you mean?" I answer as I hurry to the dresser, pull out fresh panties and slip into them.

"Well…tell me about you and Bobby last night? What was *that* all about?" Glory Ann waits as I grab a dress out of the closet and begin to put it on over my pink slip.

"*That* was nothing," I finally answer, "What do you mean? We just talked, it was nothing."

I smirked then as I look in Glory Ann's direction, although I can't look directly at my big sister. I know Glo can read my eyes, and I am in no mood to deal with that this morning. I am late already but Glory Ann doesn't care about that. She would have keep me here all day to get her answer.

"Well…it didn't look like *nothing* last night! I saw the way you looked at him. I think you like him Marty, and I think you might even have dreamt about Bobby last night," she says in a sing-song kind of way.

"Oh Glo you are being silly, I didn't look at him in any sort of way. Now, I have got to get to work. I am late and so are you. See you later."

I grab my coat and scarf from the hook on the back of the door and without another look in Glory Ann's direction, turn and open the door to leave.

"Good bye, Glo. See you tonight," I shout as I leave the apartment.

Joe, the elevator boy, opens the gate after the elevator arrives on the second floor.

"Good morning Miss Martha.," he sings as he firmly holds open the door.

"Good morning, Joe" I mimic back as best I can.

The loud elevator takes me to the lobby where I exit the building. Turning right at the door, I walk the six blocks to work.

GLORY ANN: A FEW MINUTES LATER...

"Could Martha and Bob really like each other?" Glory Ann asks herself. "Certainly not!" she decides after a quick moment. "Martha isn't Bobby's type.

I have known Bobby for several months now and I know his type. He likes the tall, blonde, outgoing girls that laugh at his jokes and giggle when he speaks and are fun, lots of fun. Marty is NOT fun. He is all about fun, laughter , noise and parties. She is nothing like the things he likes in a woman.

As she thinks of all those qualities, Glory Ann suddenly realizes that SHE is all of those things that Bobby likes. Why hadn't she thought of this before now? They have been friends for awhile now and they always spend the weekends together. They go to clubs, restaurants or picnics with their gang of friends. It never crossed her mind to date Bob.

"Maybe I am the girl for Bobby, not Martha, " she thinks to herself. "Hmmm." she says as she allows that thought to settle in her mind. "It is a possibility, a real possibility," she decides and says aloud.

BOBBY: NOVEMBER 1943

Lying here in my bunk after a busy weekend in the city, I should be tired. Usually, on the train back to the base at the end of the weekend I am beat, and sleep, but not last night. As I rode the train from NYC to Norfolk, I was wide-awake.

I love my life. I work at the naval yard during the week doing what I love, and then I ride the train to NYC every weekend to hang out with the guys from the base and the beautiful gals we meet in the city. What fun we always have. The "Y" is a great place to stay and military guys get a great rate. It is close to everything, but most importantly, to the girls' apartment. The girls are great. Each one of them is great-looking and a whole lot of fun. I have known all of them for five months now.

I even dated a couple of them for a short time, but we remain friends. It is good, predictable, and fun…always a lot of fun.

But then there was last night. It was not predictable at all. Something was different, very different for me. I can't sleep now because of it. Why had meeting Martha affected me in this way?

I had noticed her a few weeks before, right after she moved in. I met her briefly then in passing but hadn't really talked to her, until last night. Then I did it; I finally met Marty. I talked to her and she talked to me, and then I made a fool of myself.

I can't stop thinking about her. She is a tiny little thing, so tiny that if a strong wind blew up, she could get caught in it and perhaps be blown away. Her waist is so small that I could have put my hands around it and my fingers would have touched.

She has huge dark brown eyes that are too big for her tiny face. They looked at me last night with a sparkle and a shyness that drew me in, like giant pools of moving water beckoning me closer.

Her skin is so pale and flawless that I just wanted to reach out and lightly touch her cheek.

And her hair! She has long bangs that touch her eyebrows and gobble up her lashes when she opens her eyes wide. The deep auburn color and the long, thick, shining waves that hang around her shoulders and move ever so slightly as she turns held me entranced.

She has a beauty mark below her red lips that moves when she smiles. She is very unsure of herself and so shy that I just want to hold her to tell that it would be all right. She is absolutely beautiful.

I can't quit thinking about her. Why does this girl haunt me so? She is not my type. I am attracted to blondes and girls with long legs, big mouths and even bigger voices. I am not attracted to the shy, quiet, dark-haired girls. I never had been. What is it about her?

As I think of our short conversation from the night before, I remember that I had decided to follow her as she scurried across the small apartment heading to the kitchen from her room. She never hung out with the gang. She was always in her room or gone. If I saw her it was only as she was going to the kitchen for water or a snack or heading out the front door. She never sat and talked with the group. She never even looked in my direction. I just hadn't been able to understand that.

Everyone is always attracted to me and notice me, partly because I am loud, but I am friendly too. I never meet a stranger. I love being with people and love talking to anyone about anything.

Yet here was this quiet girl, drifting silently across the room. No one noticed her and she noticed no one. But for some reason, I noticed her last night and wanted suddenly to know her.

As she was reaching in the refrigerator for a drink I got up from the couch and approached her. I stood behind her as she was peering inside the fridge. As she grabbed a drink from the refrigerator she turned and ran right into me. I apologized and backed up.

She immediately looked to the floor and said, "Oh, I am sorry, sorry." Then she turned to walk to her room.

It was then that I grabbed her arm and said, "Marty, I am Bobby. It's nice to meet you," or something like that. I actually forgot what the exact words were because when she looked up into my eyes I was mesmerized by her dark eyes and perfect face. I remembered studying her face for what seemed like a very long time and she seemed to be doing the same to mine. Perhaps that is why I can remember every detail of her.

"Nice to meet you too," she replied, and then she said that she had to get back to her drawing before the ink dried.

"Oh, you're an artist?" I questioned.

"Yes, I work for a greeting card company. I have a deadline of tomorrow morning and have to finish many designs tonight. I have to go,"

I remember the panic in my stomach, a feeling that I rarely ever have. I asked if I could see her cards, wanting our short time together to stretch out some.

"Oh, you don't want to see them," she replied back.

"Yes, Yes I do!" I remembered saying to her. So, she turned then and I followed her into her room.

She walked across the room to the little desk by the window and turned as she pointed to the cards on the top of the desk. I looked at her with the light streaming through her dark hair. I remembered thinking then how very beautiful she was.

Getting somewhat flustered, I glanced at her work and back at her. Then I said the stupidest thing I had ever said to a woman.

"You are beautiful. I mean…. THEY are beautiful." Trying to cover my slip of tongue, I picked up one of the wet cards and smudged the ink all over the side of it. Then, as I was trying to wipe it off, I dropped it onto another card and ruined that one as well.

"Oh no!" I remember screaming.

Martha touched my hand ever so gently and said that it was all right, but then said I better go. She was smiling up at me with a whimsical smile, but I was so embarrassed at that point that I turned and walked out of the room.

Before I left though, I looked back at her again, and closed her door. I then sought the safety and security of my friends and that was it. I had been a total idiot and ruined two of her greeting cards. I hadn't even told her I was sorry.

No woman had ever made me feel nervous or stupid, but Martha had. I couldn't put my finger on it, but there was this crazy spell she had over me. A spell that was unpredictable and unnerving and wonderful all at the same time. I decided in that moment, sitting on the couch with my friends, that I would ask Marty out on a date. And for once in my life, I felt nervous and shy and unsure of myself.

GLORY ANN: THE NEXT WEEKEND

Bobby is coming with the boys again this weekend and I am going to give it a whirl. I am attracted to him and know that if I try, Bobby will be attracted to me as well. I am, after all, his type. Martha is not. Plus, I saw him first, he is my friend, and I AM the oldest. I always get first pick of everything. Mom makes sure of that. In this case, I know that I would work my wiles on him and he will come around, like it should be. I will make him forget my little sister. I am confident that it will never work out between Marty and Bobby.

Glory Ann worked all afternoon making herself into what she knew Bobby would like. She curled her blonde bob, painted her face and nails to perfection and even wore her new tight-fitting pink sweater. She completed her look with a shorter than normal skirt and high-heeled shoes to show off her long legs.

SEVERAL HOURS LATER...

Glory Ann worked hard to make it all happen. It wasn't long before her roommates came in from the train and plopped on the sofa next to her, chatting about their busy day at work and complaining about the cold. Then they noticed her and how she was so dressed up.

"Well..."Chloe said, "What are you so dolled up about? Trying to get a man, huh?"

The others laughed and Glory Ann smiled as if to say, *you bet your last dollar I am.*

"Who are you trying to catch, Glo?" they all wanted to know.

"I have my sights on Bobby,"

"Ohhh," they said in unison, "He is a nice catch...what got into you?"

"Oh nothing," she responded, "I just decided that I liked him and wanted to throw the nets out there this weekend and see if I could haul in a big catch. Give me my space, girls. I have work to do," she said with a wink.

With that, the door flung open and Bobby, Lloyd, Phil and Doug plowed through the door looking for fun.

Glory Ann could tell that Bobby noticed her right away. He told her immediately how very beautiful she looked. He even came over to her and put his hand on her back, rubbed it because the sweater felt soft, and then kissed Glory Ann on the cheek. She smiled, batted her long lashes, and kissed him lightly on the lips knowing that her plan was already working.

"Well, that was nice," Bobby joked after the short kiss ended and then slugged Lloyd in his ribs.

Lloyd and Bobby proceeded to jostle in the living room as they loosened their ties, got beer from the fridge, and sat on the sofa. Bob looked around the apartment then for Martha. She was nowhere to be seen, not even in her room.

"Hey, Glo," he asked, "Where is your sister?" Trying not to be jealous of Bobby's interest in Martha, Glory Ann told him that she had to work tonight at the tie store down the block. They were having some big sale and it would be late before she got home.

"Oh" he replied a little disappointed.

As the group chatted about their evening plans, Bobby kept thinking of Martha. He drank another swig of his beer and walked to the window.

"Which way is the shop?" he asked in Glory Ann's direction.

"What shop?" she asked.

"The one where Marty works."

Surprised that Bobby was still talking about Martha, Glory Ann grimaced a little and said, "It is to the left down three blocks."

Without another word, Bob turns from the window, buttons his top button on his shirt, straightens his tie, and says, " I will catch up with you guys later, I have somewhere to go."

Putting his bottle on the table next to Glory Ann, he leaves the apartment, almost skipping out the door.

Bobby was happy, really happy, and so looked forward to seeing Marty again. As he approached the shop, he glanced into the window.

He couldn't see her, so he opened the door and went in. Seeing her in the rear of the shop, Bobby started thumbing through a table of ties towards the front of the store.

Martha saw Bobby from behind and walked over, not recognizing him. She asked if she could help find the perfect tie. Bobby turned to see her as he smiled the biggest, brightest and best smile he could muster, recognizing her timid voice.

"Oh Bobby, it's you. How are you? What are you doing here? Do you need a tie?" Martha asked stumbling over her words.

All the questions came tumbling out of her mouth and landed in front of her in a heap.

Bobby didn't speak. he just kept smiling.

Her shyness overcame her and she backed up and moved her eyes to the floor.

Bobby gently reached for her chin and pulled it upward. As he did, she lifted her eyes to his. They looked deeply into each other's eyes for a very long minute. The soft brown endless pools of her eyes stirred something deep within his soul. In that moment Bobby knew he had found what he had dreamed of and longed for. And he knew she felt the same.

CHAPTER 7

LAKESIDE: SEPTEMBER, 2006

THREE GROWN DAUGHTERS SIT BEFORE Martha now. The same three daughters that Martha had once only dreamt about. She had wanted them more than anything else in the world. Only now, Martha didn't know them. The three hold her hands in theirs. Those arthritic hands are wrinkled and worn now, showing evidence of the work she had done for them over her lifetime. These same hands that painstakingly colored each announcement for their births, and the same ones that had written out each of their names time and time again. With these hands she had beautifully hand–made many outfits for them.

In Martha's mind she has three daughters. In her mind they are only babies playing together, wearing matching dresses. She knows and loves those daughters, not the three sitting before her. After all, the three before her are middle-aged women! The three daughters from her past, fill her thoughts now, and she is happy, fulfilled, and needed.

Sitting before their mother and hearing her talk of her daughters is hard, and very odd, for Leslie, Susan and Marcee. She talks of them as if they are somewhere else. In fact, they are. They are from another time and from another place, a place found only in the recesses of her mind.

The sisters hold on hoping for recognition, but that recognition doesn't come. The recognition never comes.

Out of love for their mother, Martha's daughters have to let go. Releasing their grip on the familiar word, "Mom" and replacing it with "Martha" is one of the hardest things they had to do. As difficult as it is for them, they smile at her, fighting the tears that fill their eyes. Their thoughts now are of her happiness, not their own needs.

The three middle aged ladies sit with Martha, as her acquaintances, and listen to her happily talk of her three wonderful and beautiful little girls.

MARTHA: OCTOBER, 1953

Bob and I wanted children. So much so that from the time we were first married, on our honeymoon, we tried to get pregnant. For seven long years we tried. But as luck would have it, and God's will notwithstanding, we did not get pregnant.

I began to feel depressed. To fight off feelings of despair and to occupy my time while Bob was away on deployment, I knitted pink baby booties and then blue ones on wooden toothpicks. With each microscopic stitch that I knitted, a prayer would go out from my lips for a baby.

Sometimes I would call on my greeting card experience and draw special birth announcements for our future baby girl or boy. I would painstakingly water-coloring each announcement that I drew. Those announcements remained bundled together in a closed drawer awaiting the big announcement that I prayed would come.

I pondered long and hard over names for our babies and then wrote those little names in every font I could imagine. All this I did in an attempt to bring a change in our luck, or a change to God's mind. That change finally happened.

I hear the words from the doctor that I had imagined in my mind over and over again. I am going to be a mother! I am overjoyed! I spend all my time readying the baby's room and preparing the clothes, diapers, bottles, and bedding for the new little one that will soon fill our lives. Carefully, Bob and I pick out that special name. Our first child, Marcee is born a healthy baby girl in October of 1953. This blonde, curly-headed, gray-eyed baby girl that had been wanted for so long occupies my mind every waking moment. We are very happy.

MARTHA: DECEMBER, 1955

Two years after our first child is born, Bob and I are blessed to become pregnant with our second child. This child is born a healthy baby girl, in late December. Bob and I are completely obsessed and happy with our dark-haired, dark-eyed "number two daughter," as Bob lovingly calls her. I busy myself sewing matching dresses for my two sweet girls. I feel wonderful and needed and worthwhile. I have two little girls that need and want me.

MARTHA: JULY, 1959

It is a hot day in July, when our number three daughter joins the family. She is born a beautiful, healthy little baby with strawberry blonde hair and blue eyes. Bob and I are thrilled with the addition of a third daughter making our family complete. Our three little girls, each so different, are perfect in our eyes.

MARTHA: JUNE 1977

Three daughters. I wanted and needed them so badly. I provided well for my daughters; making most of their clothes, seeing to it that they ate healthful meals, and keeping the house clean and orderly for my family. I am devoted to my daughters.

But, as my three girls grew, with age they became more independent. With their independence, my devotion changes to worry and self-doubt. I am convinced that my daughters don't need me or want me any longer.

I begin to feel worthless and not needed by any of them. I long for the time of their childhood, when I provided for all their needs. I fear that they will stray from me, not needing or wanting me any longer.

MARTHA: FALL 1982

This fear of losing my daughters encompasses me now. I don't feel needed or wanted any longer. I can't stand being alone with myself. I don't know what I am going to do with my time.

My mother's words haunt me now more than ever before. "Nothing will ever come from you, Martha, by following your passions." Those words ring true to me now and I believe them. I can't allow myself the luxury of focusing on my passions. I must stay out of myself and focus on something or someone else. But, where do I turn?

With these thoughts flooding my mind, I see Bob watching television. Focusing on his perfection, and on my imperfection, I find a renewed purpose.

CHAPTER 8

LAKESIDE: JANUARY 2006

I T WAS 6:10 AM, TIME for Kathy to be at work. The night shift of caregivers would leave at 6:30 and she had to check with each of them to see how her beloved residents had done the night before. Five of the residents were sundowners who walked and remained busy throughout the night. She was running late, as usual and hated it.

Her old station wagon clanked and chugged the 15 miles it had to trudge to get to Lakeside. Each day, her worry was the same. Would this old, run down car make it to work today? She prayed so. Most days her prayers were answered and for that she was glad. She didn't have the money to replace the hand-me-down car, so it *had* to make it.

Arriving at work, Kathy grabbed her scrubs from the passenger seat, locked her car and ran up the stairs to the back door.

As she arrived that morning she glanced at the bulletin board to see what was important in her residents' lives for that day. She saw that today was Doris's birthday. She ran into the kitchen, and unlocked her office door. She threw her purse onto her desk and turned to see Doris entering the room.

"Hi sweet lady," she spoke. "Today is a very special day, isn't it?" Doris looked at her and smiled.

Kathy reached for Doris' hand and looked into her dancing, child-like eyes and said, "It is your birthday today!"

Doris smiled once again and nodded in agreement. Kathy hugged the elderly woman and kissed her on the cheek.

"We are going to have a party today! Where is Martha? Have you told her it is your birthday, yet?" Kathy asked.

"Yes," whispered Doris. Kathy knew that Doris had not told Martha. In fact, Kathy was well aware that in just a few minutes, after their conversation was over, Doris would forget altogether that it was her own birthday.

"Let's see, Doris, how old are you?" Kathy inquired, not expecting an answer.

She glanced at the poster on the other side of the room on the bulletin board knowing she would find her answer on it. There in the spotlight was Doris' poster. It was hanging in the space reserved for the resident of the month. Since it was Doris's birthday this month, she had been chosen. Kathy asked Doris's family to make her poster.

Kathy read the poster quickly and admired the black and white photo of Doris smiling so sweetly with her daughters and husband gathered around her. It was the same smile Kathy had received that morning, the one Doris still wore every day.

There above the photo was Doris's birth date and another photo of her as a small child.

"Feb. 12, 1930," she read. "Do you remember, Doris? That is your birthday. So, you are…" Kathy paused for a moment quickly doing the math in her head, "seventy-six years old today, Doris!" She squeezed the older woman's hand as she spoke.

"Yes," Doris replied.

Unlike some of the residents, Doris only had a few words left in her vocabulary. She had forgotten most words. She spoke mostly through her eyes and smiles. Kathy knew Doris's unique language so well that she only had to look at her expression to know what Doris needed or felt. She always knew what the sweet lady was thinking at any given moment.

"What a party we are going to have today, my friend!" Kathy smiled knowing that Doris loved parties.

As the women exited the kitchen, Kathy spoke the few words that Doris still remembered, "I love you, Doris," meaning it with every fiber in her being.

"I love you too," Doris mimicked.

Kathy knew Doris meant it and hugged her, living in the moment, because that moment would soon pass and Doris would not remember it.

Kathy led Doris into the Gathering Room as she slipped into the kitchen once again to get ready for her day. Her small office, just big enough for a small desk and chair, was conveniently located in a closet adjacent to the kitchen. She went into her office and sat down. This time would probably be the last that she would be able to sit for the rest of the day.

She scanned the calendar on her desk to see what was planned for today. Elvis Day and Doris's birthday were neatly written in the square for that day.

Elvis Day was always fun for the residents. They would make peanut butter and banana sandwiches, Elvis's favorite, together in the kitchen. They would eat while listening to Elvis records. The caregivers would encourage the residents to even get up and dance to the beat of the familiar tunes. Music was so important at Lakeside and it filled the halls as often as time would allow. Most of the residents would be able to recall the old tunes that they once loved and then would sing along.

Some of Kathy's caregiver staff would dress like Elvis wearing dark sunglasses and tight jumpsuits. They would slick-back their hair and put on a long glittering scarf dangling from their necks. Doris and Martha would love today, and would probably want to dress up too.

Kathy closed her office door to greet the residents for breakfast. An outsider looking around Kathy's messy office would immediately assume that she was very disorganized and unkempt, but they would be wrong.

There was clutter everywhere except on top of her calendar which filled the top of her desk. The walls were filled with artwork, photographs, bible verses and "stuff." She had accumulated so much of it over the last year or so working at Lakeside that there wasn't an inch left of the cheerful yellow that she had painted on her walls when she had started.

Piled in each corner of the little room were craft supplies, CD's, costumes, and props. There was even a little broken chair in the corner. There was no closet space upstairs in Memory Care so her office was the closet as well as her private space. She didn't mind. She absolutely loved every piece that cluttered the walls of the small office.

When she had a free moment, which was rare, she would sit in her chair and look at each piece and remember Patrice or Homer or John or Olivia. Each one of them, and many others, held a very special place in her heart and each one was part of her family. Some of them had been difficult residents, but she loved them just the same. Others were so special to her that when they passed, she could not bear the hurt and would spend hours searching for a bible verse that would help to ease her pain. Then, after it was found, she would hang that verse on her wall, usually on top of something else, so she could read and reread it again and again.

Kathy had some of Martha's artwork on her wall. She knew that Martha loved to paint; it was one of her joys. Sometimes what Martha painted actually resembled whatever she had told Kathy it was, and sometimes not. Kathy made sure to jot down what Martha had said it was somewhere on the painting. Color was something Martha loved and so her paintings were always colorful and bright. The artist inside Martha escaped from her inner self almost weekly as they had painting time.

Right next to her desk hung a photo someone took of Doris, Martha, and Kathy all wearing colorful boas around their necks. They had been dancing to the tunes of Mitch Miller, one of Martha's favorites. Doris enjoyed anything that Martha enjoyed and they were inseparable. Their friendship was unique and special. Kathy was amazed at the friendship that they formed so shortly after Martha's arrival at Lakeside.

Kathy tried very hard not to have favorites, but Doris and Martha remained two women that Kathy would love forever and never forget.

Martha, now she is a rare one, Kathy thinks. Martha is filled with so much joy and happiness and love inside her that it bubbles out in all sorts of ways. Oh how she wished she had known Martha as a young woman. She knows that they would have been the best of friends. Kathy is sure there are many people from Martha's life that miss her lively and fun spirit.

Kathy realizes once again that she is blessed. She is able to spend every day with Martha, Doris and the other residents and she loves it.

CHAPTER 9

LAKESIDE: FEBRUARY 2006

KATHY OPENED THE CLOSET AND brought out a large, shiny, box. One might say it was rather gaudy actually. It was adorned with every color plastic jewel and ribbon that Kathy could find at the dollar store. There were sequins, bric-a-brac, and even flashy stickers in some spots. It looked to be a box that a kindergarten class had decorated.

When she found the old box after cleaning out a forgotten closet one day, she decided to have a craft day with it. The residents loved crafts and they loved surprises even more, so decorating the box together and then putting something special inside for them to find was especially fun.

A lid sat snuggly on the top, waiting there for eager eyes and minds to wonder what was inside. Kathy set it on the table and stood back to see what the residents would do. This ritual was repeated several times a week and the wonder of it never ceased to amaze the well-trained caregiver.

Some of the residents were curious and walked over to the box right away. Other residents would look at the box for some time and then slowly, one after the other would get up and come over to the box and look at it. Some would reach out and touch it. Most of them didn't recognize the gaudy box.

They would start to discuss amongst themselves what treasure it might contain. After a few minutes of this part of the game, Kathy then would ask the residents what they thought was inside. By this time most of the residents would have gathered around the table.

"It's a present," said Edna, "Is it my birthday?"

"No, not today," Kathy would say every time the box was shown.

Every time the box came out one of the residents would think it was their birthday.

"A treasure," Beatrice exclaimed excitedly.

"No" replied Margaret angrily from the next room. "We all know, it is the jewelry!" she would say in a matter-of-fact way.

Each time they played this guessing game, different ideas would surface. Margaret always got it right. Margaret remembered the box and what it contained.

As Kathy slowly opened the box, the residents got very excited. They all leaned in close to peer inside the secret box to see the treasure inside.

Kathy slowly, very slowly, started to pull out the contents, pausing as she went, just to make it more exciting. The first item lifted from the top was a beautiful sparkling bracelet. She asked who wanted to wear it. One of the ladies said, "I do!" After placing the bracelet on the first woman's arm, she proceeded to take out each of the gaudy pieces of jewelry one after the other. She placed each on one of the ladies' wrists, neck or finger.

All the residents loved the jewels. Each lady admired her piece and then had a story to tell of how she obtained her jewel. Usually it was a long ago memory that had been stored away, brought to the surface once again. One would speak of the gift her husband had given her on their wedding day. Another would say it was from her mother or boyfriend or sister. With each of these special memories came smiles and laughter. Some didn't have a story or memory, but loved the sparkles nonetheless.

As they admired each other's jewelry, some of the ladies would glance around like a spy and then sneak their jewel into their pocket, unaware that they were under the watchful eyes of the caregivers. Others would travel back to their room, to hide their treasure in a secret place. Each time the box was pulled out, some of the pieces would disappear, showing up later in the washing machine, or on a night stand, or at the dinner table. Sometimes, the pieces were never seen again, hiding forever in a cleverly thought out hiding place.

Martha usually wore the same ring. She would wait until the diamond was pulled from the box and stake her claims on it exclaiming to anyone that would ask, "Bob gave it to me!"

With a broad smile on her face, Martha would drift off into a memory of him and then his words, spoken to her so long ago, would surface in her mind, "Think of me when you wear this ring, and I will be with you forever." Sometimes she repeated those words aloud to herself and sometimes she kept them private, but, she always remembered them. With those special words spoken so long ago, he was there with her in her heart and mind.

BOB: SPRING 1965

Wandering through the narrow streets of Barcelona I stumble across a tiny nondescript shop while looking for a ring for Martha. I sit on the bench waiting for the shop to open as I reflect on my navy career.

Martha and the girls and I have enough money to live comfortably. During my time in the Navy I have been deployed to many exciting places around the world. One place in particular that I enjoy visiting is this romantic seaport of Barcelona. I feel comfortable wandering these streets alone as I have been here many times over the years.

In my travels to these foreign ports, I am always on the lookout for gifts for the girls. I have found dolls, clothes, furniture, rugs and one time, I even brought home a spanish-speaking parrot. But my favorite gifts to find, and the ones I enjoy searching for the most, are special pieces of jewelry for Martha. I am proud of the collection of rings,necklaces and looses stones that I have brought her from around the world.

The shop owner arrives momentarily and we begin to discuss some of his wares. Soon I spy a ring in a small case and ask my new friend if I can see it. As the man pulls the ring from the case, I know it is special. It's called a princess ring. It is adorned with many small stones, each a different type. There are rubies, sapphires, emeralds, and amethysts. On the very top of the heap of stones is a larger diamond. I am fascinated by this ring and have to have it. The haggling begins and I finally get the shop owner down to a reasonable price. Putting it safely into my pocket, I make my way back to the ship at the dock. My Navy career has been good to me.

MARTHA: SUMMER 1965

Standing on the little knoll with my daughters surrounding me, I look towards the sea. I feel the warm ocean breeze blowing my hair and skirt as I try to focus on the distant speck on the horizon. Taking my large white sunglasses from my eyes, I cup my hand over my brow trying to focus in even closer. Recognizing the speck as the ship, I know it won't be long before the ship arrives, bringing my Bob back to me. I have longed for this moment and have waited for it for seven long months for this day to come. The ship steams toward the shore and moves past my little secret spot here on the knoll.

I love this spot. I found it several cruises ago and have come to it ever since to watch and wait for my Bob to return to me. The few minutes spent here alone with my thoughts of him are my favorite moments before seeing him again.

Bob, my only love, is almost with me and an uncontrollable smile spreads across my face. My thoughts race to him; his special smile he has just for me, the twinkle in his eye upon seeing me for the first time again, and his lips that will envelope mine, all filled my thoughts now. I love him so much that it aches. I have slept in his t-shirt every night since he left. His smell is long gone from it, but I still remember. Oh how I long for his smell again.

I am forced from my daydream as Leslie squeals in delight when she too sees the boat on the water. I look out to see the ship steaming toward us, much more than a speck now. Time seems to slip into the sea as the ship carrying my life steams forward towards home.

As the massive ship slides past my little secret spot, I know I wouldn't be able to see Bob yet. He is hidden on the bridge with the Captain. Many of the sailors are on deck performing the last minute chores necessary before the ship pulls into the port. Upon seeing the other men, joy leaps from my heart and mind, and the girls and I jump up and down and wave at the destroyer. Most of the men were busily readying the ship for docking, but a few men turn towards us to wave and smile at our little family on the hill. Quickly, the ship slides past our vantage point on the knoll and is out of sight.

As the ship cruises past, I grab Leslie's hand and the four of us run to the station wagon parked not far away. I drive down to join the others on the dock to celebrate the ship's return.

I know that the next few hours will be the hardest. I will have to wait with the other families until their fathers, sons, husbands and brothers disembark.

The first men off the ship are the new dads. I love this special ritual and so does everyone there. The sight of these new dads running to their wives, who were holding their new babies is very heart-warming.

These men could not be at the births of their children and having never met their little ones before, it is fitting that they get to be the first off the boat.

After the new fathers are off the ship the rest of the crew can leave. All of the families have been waiting for hours for their loved ones. They carry balloons, posters, and flags. It is always such a joyous crowd, full of celebration. With ten thousand people meeting the ship, each family decides on a meeting place beforehand. Trying to find one's family in that crowd is nearly impossible if the meeting spot isn't decided beforehand. My Bob, the Executive Officer and second in command, is always one of the last to leave the ship. So, we wait.

After several hours of watching and waiting, Bob, my Executive Officer, finally descends from the ship. As he walks down the brow, the sky above his head glows bright red and orange, signaling the end of a long day. In his hands he carries a bag. Upon seeing us, Bob drops his bag and runs to the girls. I watch lovingly as he hugs and kisses each one. He tells them how big they have gotten, and how much he missed them.

Finally, he looks up at me, and smiles my smile. Seeing that familiar smile, meant only for me, I melt. His outstretched arms embrace me and I cave into him. As he draws me closer, he wraps his arms tightly around me giving me the security and power I so need and have longed for. As the strength flows from his body to mine, I am complete and happier than he could ever know.

When our family gets home, it is late, but our girls know they won't have to go to bed until their daddy pulls his treasures from his bag. He hands each of the girls a doll to put on their shelf, adding it to their growing collection. They each get a scarf and an inlaid wooden jewelry box. A handmade purse for each of them is the final gift from their father.

As the girls scurry to their rooms to place their treasures away, Bob turns to me. Taking a beautifully wrapped box out of his bag, he kisses me gently. He hands the box to me and sits back to enjoy the scene.

I open the box to find the most gorgeous ring I have ever seen. Looking at Bob, I gingerly pull the ring from the box and let him place it on my finger. It fits perfectly. I love that ring, mostly because Bob had picked it out especially for me.

As he places the ring on my finger, he looks deep into my eyes and says, "Think of me whenever you wear this ring, and I will be with you forever."

I know that I will remember these special words until the end of time.

CHAPTER 10

LAKESIDE: MARCH, 2006

SHERI, THE HOUSEKEEPER, POPPED IN and out of all the resident's rooms every day cleaning, making or changing the beds, and picking up the laundry. The job was much more to her though; it was a blessing, and she was a blessing to the residents too. She would jabber happily in her southern drawl to all the residents as she straightened, cleaned and tidied up the apartments.

Every day Sheri pushed around a big cart containing all her supplies, but also containing a vast and every-changing array of throw pillows, shawls, stuffed animals, photos, greeting cards, costume jewelry and even the occasional baby doll. With her tiny one hundred pound frame and her overloaded cart, Sheri ended up looking like a street person carting around all her precious possessions.

She knew each of the resident's rooms well. She knew which items belonged in each room and which didn't. Without commotion, Sheri would silently sneak any displaced items onto her cart and place them back in the proper rooms. She did this chore on a daily basis without caring that it wasn't in her job description.

Sheri remembered the first day she met Martha. Martha hadn't been at Lakeside very long, and she had seemed depressed and tried to remain alone in her room. Sheri knew she had her job cut out for her with this one. Martha would be a tough nut to crack, but Sheri was determined and would not give up until she had gotten to know all about this sad woman.

One day, Martha was in her room sulking about one thing or another, so Sheri sat next to Martha on the bed and talked to her. Sheri's motto always was, "Talk is cheap," and Sheri could talk. Something about her simple nature drew relaxation and conversation from people, especially from Martha. Sheri knew that to be her gift. So, she sat there and asked Martha questions...questions about her life, her husband, her children, and her passions.

After several days with her new friend, Martha's tongue loosened and she slowly began to trust Sheri and answer her questions. With each visit, she would speak more freely.

Martha spoke about Bob most of the time at the beginning, so it got to where Sheri would come in every day and ask her how Bob was doing, which always seemed to lift Martha's spirits. Martha would talk on and on about Bob or the Navy. At this point, in her mind Martha didn't have children so Bob was her life.

Sheri would look through all Martha's photos whenever she came for a visit. There were lots of pictures of Bob and Martha as young adults. Bob would be wearing his uniform in most of them, and Sheri would always mention how handsome he was. She would sit on the bed and look and look at the photos with Martha.

The longer Martha stayed at Lakeside, the less she talked about Bob, and Sheri would remind her who he was and what he did. Then Martha would remember.

Sheri began taking Martha with her on her rounds sometimes to fold towels or dust the tables with her. Martha loved to help. Martha liked to stay busy. It made her happy.

She was comfortable with Sheri and enjoyed her company. Sheri provided her with the security and strength that she needed, and somehow Sheri knew that, so Martha became her helper. It got to where Martha would wait anxiously at her door for Sheri, hardly able to contain her happiness when the woman she loved rounded the corner. Perhaps Sheri filled a void somewhere deep within her. When asked about her, Martha would say that Sheri was sweet. Sheri was her friend.

When Martha was close to the end, Sheri came and sat on her bed and talked to Martha about Bob. She held her hand, while her own tears dampened the same sheets she had washed, folded and straightened for her sweet friend, Martha. The only words Martha said to her that last day was, "Thank you Sheri for getting me through the summers with its long days and longer nights". Martha loved her friend, Sheri, and Sheri loved her.

MARTHA: SUMMER 1968

The summers are the worst. Once again I have to endure another summer without Bob, as the Navy has separated our family once again. I hate summer because all the days are so long. Each day drags on into the next. Darkness, and the end of my day, come so late now. I can't bear the loneliness of the longer days. Dusk is the absolute least favorite part of my day with its grays and shades of darkness creeping into the shadows, making everything appear the same. I can't really sense color anymore.

The girls play in the background of my thoughts and the disharmony of the sounds invade me.

Sherry is my friend, my comforter. I crave its sweet taste on my lips. It takes me to a time I long for in my life. As the first glass of wine is finished, I methodically put each plate at its proper place on the table, readying for dinner. The girls will occupy the same seats in the dining room, chattering relentlessly about their day. Sipping on my sherry, I can make it through their babbling and will be thankful when the meal comes to an end.

After dinner, as the girls clear the table and load the dishwasher, I retreat to the living room anxiously arriving on the couch. Mitch Miller is playing on the stereo.

As the screen door slams shut, I realize my daughters have gone out to play again. Thankful, I carefully walk to the kitchen to refill my glass. Grabbing my cigarettes from the drawer and with ashtray in hand, I head to my retreat once more.

Dusk is approaching and I need my armor to be ready. I long for the day's battle to be over. With every thought that creeps into my mind, I take another sip of sherry to erase the ever-present pain I feel. The moments fade as my eyes close and I allow sleep to carry me away.

MARCEE: AN HOUR LATER...

As darkness invades the sky and the daylight disappears, so too, do the happy thoughts within my mind. As I open the front door, the music from within masks the sad thoughts that are racing through my head. Gone is the daytime, with its normalcy and hope, replaced by the nightmare that greets me at the door. My nightly routine is ready to unfold. Without looking at my mother sleeping on the couch, I ready my sisters for bed. The water glasses are filled, the prayers recited, and the hugs are given. I complete these same tasks each night.

As I finally can focus on Mom, the familiar scene is etched once again into my memory. I pick up the lipstick-rimmed glass and the burning cigarette, and with utter loathing, place them methodically in their proper places in the kitchen.

I sit on the floor next to my mother's head, coaxing her to get up. Mom stirs angrily, grumbling under her breath as she pushes me away. I continue my struggle as I lift my mother from the couch.

We proceed down the hall with my mother's protests becoming childlike, reversing our roles. Pulling the covers around my mother's shoulders, I am relieved to know the day is over. I creep out of the room and shut the door on my way. I lock the front door, turn off the lights and whisper good night to Mitch as I switch off the stereo.

Climbing the stairs to my room, I know that daylight will bring more hope and one less day with my Dad out to sea.

MARCEE: SPRING 1969

Mom is at it again, I think as I prolonged my time in the kitchen doing the dishes. *Another night, another fight.* I wonder if I can slip off to my room without anyone noticing me.

Most nights, I count the glasses she drinks. It is always four or five, sometimes even six. I don't know why I have to count, but I do.

At least when Dad is home I am not in charge, so I let Dad take care of her. That is a relief of sorts. Dad usually gets frustrated with her and ends up going to bed mad. We all do.

The monster comes out at night. During the day, Mom is Mom. She is pleasant, busy, and caring. It's like this beast, hiding within her comes out after five o'clock, taking over her body and our house. After that, not one of us can be normal. Once the picture–perfect dinner is over, the messed up family emerges with this creature that I don't know, in charge.

I don't blame Dad. I don't even blame Mom. Now that I am older, I know it is not my fault or my sisters' fault. She is just so unhappy. I figure that deep down inside, she doesn't think she is worthy of her family or a normal life. She drinks to forget her pain. She takes depression medicine and has for a long time. I don't think it is working. I pray that I can slip by her tonight and not have our usual confrontation.

Susan always tells me, "Just be quiet and let her say whatever she wants 'cause she won't remember any of it in the morning anyways."

But, I can't be quiet, she makes me mad and I end up saying what I think.

Sometimes, even Dad gets mad at me because he doesn't think I am showing respect to my mother. I don't understand how he can say that? How can I be respectful when she doesn't even respect herself. She wouldn't do this night after night, if she did. I spent many years putting my mother to bed while he was at sea; I had to be the parent then and I have lost all patience with her.

So tonight, ever so slowly and quietly, I slip around the den trying not to be seen by them, praying as I go that tonight will be different.

MARCEE: WINTER 2004

One of the first places we have to go when Mom comes to visit is the liquor store. We go to the liquor store to purchase Mom's sherry. The shop owner orders it when she is in town. He told us a while back that not many people drink sherry anymore, at least not the young people. He knows though that when Mom is visiting he needs to order a case to have it on hand for her.

After Dad died, Mom would come up with one of my sisters or sometimes fly up for the summer to stay with me. It wasn't too difficult then to control her drinking. I would be sure to have supper ready by five-thirty or six o'clock. If I could do that, our evening would be fine because she wouldn't be able to drink much before she ate. Food in her belly was always a good thing. If for some reason we had to delay dinner, it was not good, so I avoided that as often as possible.

As her memory started getting worse, I learned a rather sneaky trick. When we bought a new bottle of sherry, I would quickly put the bottle away. It had a screw top, which was lucky for me. I could open it without her knowing. I learned I could control how much she drank without a fight.

When I had an uninterrupted minute, I would empty out most of the sherry from the bottle into a nondescript container. I would then hide that container carefully behind pots and pans that were rarely used. I would replace the cap on the bottle and put it back where she had it. Only a small amount of sherry would remain. When Mom would come to the cabinet to get her bottle at night, she would only have enough sherry to fill one glass.

She would always say the same thing, "Humph, I thought I had more sherry in here, well I have enough for one glass, that's good. We will have to go to the store tomorrow and get another bottle, O.K.?"

I would always agree. We rarely had to go to the liquor store anymore because each night, she still only had enough sherry for one glass. Her one bottle lasted a very long time. Our visits were much more pleasant that way and she didn't realize that she wasn't drinking as much.

By the time we had to put Mom in the Alzheimer's facility, she had forgotten altogether that she drank. She had forgotten the darkness within her. She had forgotten her beloved sherry, or so we thought.

CHAPTER 11

LAKESIDE: JULY 2006

MARTHA

Martha was born in July 1925. She grew up in Sunapee, New Hampshire with her parents, Edith and James, and older sister Glory Ann. Her oldest sister, Shirley died as a child. Her family owned a guesthouse, "Sleepy Hollow" that she and her sister helped run every spring and summer. She attended Pratt Art Institute in NYC where she met Robert, an ensign in the Navy. They married. Bob and Martha traveled to several seaports with the Navy for seven years until their oldest daughter, Marcee, was born in Great Lakes, Illinois in fall of 1953. They had 2 more daughters, Susan (born in Newport, R.I in 1955) and Leslie (Born in Marshfield, MA in 1959). Bob pursued his thirty year Navel career, traveling with Martha and the girls up and down the east coast of the U.S. and abroad. Bob spent a lot of time "out to sea," and Martha and the girls waited for his safe return. He served in WWII, Korea (Underwater demolition), and Vietnam. Bob retired as a Captain. Martha loves the Navy, and is very proud to be a "navy wife". During many tours of duty, Martha was the Captain's wife and would be the "mother hen" to all the wives while the ship was out to sea. She loved to take care of "her" wives. Martha loved to entertain. When Bob retired, they lived part of the year in Bradenton, Florida and spent the summers on Cape Cod, Massachusetts, where they ran a small gift shop. During retirement Martha and Bob traveled extensively in their motor home, or boat. Bob passed away after a long battle with cancer in 2002. Martha has ten Grandchildren.

AS WAS CUSTOMARY AT LAKESIDE, it was Martha's turn to be the "Resident of the Month". Marcee had made the poster telling of Martha's life for the other families to read so they could know Martha. The caregivers would read it as well and enjoyed looking at all the old photos of their charge and learn more about her. Martha was proud of her poster and on most days, stared at the photos of those she loved.

Today, as Martha stares at her poster hanging on the bulletin board, she looks at picture of Glory Ann and Stan. Martha loves her sister, Glory Ann. As Martha looks up from the picture, she sees Glory Ann through the window standing by her car waving at her. She has just arrived for a visit. Martha's heart starts pounding in her chest. She gets excited. Her big sister Glory Ann, and her husband, are here to visit with her and Bob for the week!

BOB: WINTER 1979

Glory Ann was arriving today. I knew that Martha's mind battle would start soon. Martha loved her sister so much and on one hand wanted very much to see her, but on the other, the dread of having her mind reach back into her memories of her childhood with Glory Ann and their mother, reliving them once again, would consume her.

These once-a-year visits always did the same thing to her. They brought to the surface her torturous self-loathing from deep within. She had learned to hide it most of the time, but never seemed to be able to around Glory Ann. I knew that Martha would wrestle with herself as she awaited their arrival. I didn't understand the spell her sister had over her. Martha is a grown woman with children of her own, so why did she still feel like the little sister every time Glory Ann was around?

BOB: LATER THAT EVENING...

Martha and Glory Ann exchanged all the pleasantries that people do when they greet each other after a long time. Each sister was sincere but each in very different ways. Glory Ann, once again, took control and demanded everyone's attention.

She waltzed into our living room like a princess holding her head high. She was beautiful. She looked ten years younger than she was and with this visit she looked even younger than Martha. She started taking over for her little sister immediately. She accomplished all of this before she opened her mouth.

With the very sight of her sister's proud and beautiful face and body, Martha caved. I could see it. Not only physically with her body, but I knew it happened in her mind too. In just the first few minutes, the battle had been won and "the child" Martha sat, listening with wonder to Glory Ann tell of their travels and business without saying a word besides "Oh how wonderful" and "That must have been so much fun!"

My heart hurts for Martha knowing what is going on in her mind.

I could tell that Martha listened intently to Glory Ann tell her stories of her successes, her children, and her travels. All of which added up to an exciting life. Then, finally after quite some time, Glory Ann asked how Martha was.

Martha quietly spoke to her sister as a child with a grown up voice. She told her about me, about where I had been going and what I had been doing. She talked about our girls and then asked about Glory Ann's daughters again. She spoke nothing of herself.

Glory Ann theatrically pulled every photo she had from her wallet, describing in detail each of her daughter's accomplishments. She came over next to Martha on the couch, grabbed her sister's hand and shared with her for another hour.

Martha listened patiently and quietly assumed her proper role as she held onto her sister's hand.

As time slowly moves forward, I can see in Martha's eyes that her demeanor has retreated to the place that she had dreaded.

BOB: ONE WEEK LATER…

For the rest of the week, whenever Glory Ann wasn't talking of herself and her family, she was working on Martha. She helped her pick out some beautiful new clothes at the mall, a new hair color, and gave her the usual advice on exercise and diet. Glory Ann knew what was best for Martha, and Martha listened and did as she was told.

As the visit came to its end, I knew that Glory Ann felt accomplished having helped her little sister out. Martha felt loved in a little sister sort of way. Everyone hugged and kissed goodbye as Glory Ann and Martha's eyes filled with tears.

Waving from the driveway, with the luxury cadillac pulling away, I know it will be a long, hard week ahead. As I lovingly watch my wife wave to her sister, I know that Martha is the child again. It will be a while before I have my wife back again. The battle that repeatedly rages inside her has begun and it won't be pretty. I am here to support her, but ultimately she will have to fight it herself. I pray for God's loving arms to embrace her now, as I know mine won't be enough.

MARTHA: WINTER 1979

As Glory Ann and Stan drive into the driveway, my mind succumbs once again to my inner torture. I try desperately to avoid it. As the car stops and I see her beautiful smiling face, I begin to regress into the mindset I had as a child. It is slow at first but descends with greater speed as the moments wear on. Why did Glory Ann have such control over me still? I don't know.

I can tell by her beautiful new clothes that Glory Ann and Stan's business is going very well. After all, being on television is exactly what Glory Ann should do. I know the audience loves her as much as I do. I am not surprised at all by her success. I love her and am so proud of my big sister.

Within the first hour of Glory Ann's visit, Martha quietly allows her inner child-self to reign over her adult person. She gives in once again. That is the way it is and will always be. Martha is accustomed to their familiar routine. Glory Ann is first and Martha is second. Her mother trained them well.

CHAPTER 12

LAKESIDE: OCTOBER, 2006

EACH OF MARTHA'S DAUGHTERS' HUSBANDS and her grandchildren are forgotten. They don't exist to her anymore. Even when she sees their photographs in the photo albums, Martha doesn't realize she is blessed to have them in her life.

Martha sits with her hands in her lap waiting for her friend to arrive. She knows he is supposed to come today. It will be dinnertime soon and then it will be too late. Martha gets up from her chair and goes out the door to the fenced patio.

She sits once again waiting and looking towards the parking lot. Not that she would recognize his car, but she sits with anticipation.

Rob had left work a little early that day. He planned to visit with Martha, but his day had gotten busier than he wanted so he wasn't leaving as early as he would have liked. He wondered if perhaps he had stayed busy on purpose to delay his visit a little longer. He was not looking forward to it but felt somewhere deep inside that he needed to go.

He was comfortable there when he went to visit her with Marcee. She did most of the talking, but today, it would be he and Martha alone. What would they talk about? How uncomfortable would that feel? He knew all the residents there by name. After all, he had gone there with Marcee many times and had heard all the stories about them from her.

This was the first time he was going by himself. He really dreaded it since his and Martha's relationship had never been close. It was non-existent really.

Having been married to Marcee for some thirty years, he knew Marcee's mother well. He and Martha had rarely seen eye to eye on anything over the years, and there were times when her drinking and unpleasant behavior had driven him to say some things to her that he regretted. Someday, he would ask for forgiveness.

Martha's demeanor towards him was rarely pleasant, and the way that she treated her daughters was unforgivable in Rob's eyes. So, he remained angry with her for who she was, how she had acted in the past, and what she had done to Marcee.

Rob thought back on a time some thirty years ago, when he came for his first visit to Bob and Martha's house as Marcee's husband. He was young and a good impression was important to him then. The few times he had been with her family before had been strained, they seemed distant and not interested in a relationship. He was instructed to call her parents Captain and Mrs. There was no invitation for him to consider getting close to them. Call it insecurity, but to him it seemed that Martha had always disliked him right from the beginning.

At that first visit, Marcee's sisters were there since they hadn't left home yet. Rob had been nervous but looked forward to getting to know his wife's family better. Everyone had hugged him and asked how the trip had been as the couple came in the door. All the pleasantries had been there. Rob hadn't started to realize his destiny with her family until dinnertime when they sat down to eat.

Martha made a proclamation to everyone that she was so happy to have all her girls and Bob with her and that having Marcee home made her family complete again. Rob could distinctly remember the feeling of utter rejection. Martha didn't even try to include him in the conversation or in the family for that matter. It remained that way from then on. He remained on the outside, looking in.

The visits never got much better; in fact, they got worse. So as time passed, Rob had opted out of visiting whenever he could. He never really knew why she treated him that way, and now she had Alzheimer's and there was no way amends could ever be made. He wasn't quite sure what he would encounter when visiting her one on one.

The drive was a rather short one, and he arrived and parked before five, which was dinnertime, so he had a very few minutes to visit. That was long enough for him.

Heading up the stairs, he said a little prayer that his visit would be a pleasant one. As he entered the Gathering Room, he looked around but did not see Martha there. He checked with Doris and Gertrude to no avail, so he knew that the only other place she could be was out on the patio. The day was cool and dry so the caregivers probably took some of the residents out to enjoy the fresh air today.

He went through the doorway and there, sitting with her back towards him, was his mother-in-law. He pasted a smile on his face, took a deep breath, and walked over to the waiting woman.

"Martha" he called, mustering all the excitement his voice would allow.

Martha turned her head and with clear recognition stood up and stretched her arms out to welcome Rob. As she hugged him she squealed and said, "Oh, it is so good to see you!"

Rob had never gotten that kind of welcome from her ever before. He was relieved and felt a twinge of happiness deep in his heart, still wanting her approval. She held his hand and walked with him around the little circle of chairs to introduce her "old" friend to the other residents. She was genuinely thrilled to see him and so enjoyed introducing him to her friends.

When all the introductions were made, the two sat together in chairs facing each other. Martha never let go of his hand. She smiled and talked to him of times long ago when she and Bob would come over to visit him. She laughed as she told tale after tale of the funny antics they did together.

Rob realized then that Martha thought he was an old friend, perhaps a good friend of Bob's, but definitely not her son-in-law, so he played along. Her happiness at seeing him stirred something in his soul and he was glad he had come. He decided then that he needed to make time to come to see her alone more often, and so he did.

He began to come by on his own every other week or so and continued for the next two years visiting his old friend, Martha. Although Martha already seemed to "know" him, he felt that he was finally building a relationship with her and for that he was glad. He made Martha smile and she always looked forward to his visits. He knew he was doing something good by coming.

She always said the same words to him when he was leaving.

"I love you, please come back soon to visit. You are Bob's best friend, now you are mine."

How odd it felt for him to hear those words from her. Never had he thought he would hear Martha tell him that she loved him, but it was happening and it felt good. Rob always hugged Martha and eventually he would tell her that he loved her too.

CHAPTER 13

LAKESIDE: NOVEMBER 2006

THE GIANT MAILBOX HAD BEEN carried into the Gathering Room. All the residents sat eagerly waiting for the daily mail to be distributed.

Kathy enjoyed this part of her job. She kept very close track of how many letters and cards each resident received in the mail. It was so important that each resident felt special and wanted. If one of them didn't receive a piece of mail for several days, Kathy and the other caregivers would write a card to them from their husband or daughter or son or niece or nephew. They knew all the families and so that task wasn't too hard.

As Kathy proceeded to pass out the mail on this particular day, she watched Martha. Martha received a card from one of her daughters. Martha could no longer read, as was the case with most of the residents. Kathy and the other caregivers would sit beside each resident and read their card or letter to them. Martha always said that she had read it already but Kathy knew better. This day, Martha got up from her chair and proceeded to leave the room. Kathy decided to follow her. Martha made her way to her room with the card in hand. She saw Martha take the card and lift it to her nose every few minutes.

As Martha entered her room, Kathy followed. Martha went over to the bed, lifted her mattress ever so slightly, and placed the card underneath. Seeing Martha perform this task was a surprise because Martha's queen size mattress was heavy. Sheri had mentioned this to Kathy one time but Kathy had never understood what it meant until now. With this task finished, Martha turned and left her room once again.

When Kathy returned to the Gathering Room, Martha was sitting with Doris chatting about paying for dinner. They couldn't decide who to pay and how much it should cost. Kathy sat next to Martha and asked if she got a letter today.

Martha said, "Oh yes, I did."

"Who is it from?" Kathy asked, even though she already knew what Martha would say.

"From Bob, of course."

"Oh that's sweet and why did you smell the letter from Bob?" Kathy asked her.

"Because it always smells like diesel, from the engine room on the ship. I love that smell, because it is his smell," Martha replied happily.

With those words Kathy patted Martha's hand.

"Bob will be home soon," she said.

Martha smiled and said "And I can't wait!"

MARTHA: SPRING 1950

As the sun shone brightly in the blue sky, I gaze longingly at the clouds drifting by. The wooden bench begins to get uncomfortable as I dream of the day Bob will come back to me. I can feel his presence here with me although he was a world away.

The Korean War was a complete devastation to everyone in the United States. My Bob was called up to serve in the war efforts. Bob didn't want me living alone while he was away for almost a year, so I had moved in with Glory Ann to help with the children. Glory Ann's husband, Stan, was also called to serve.

During the year that Bob was on deployment, the mailman became my best friend. I waited patiently each day for him to bring news from my Bob. The letters were few and far between, but I cherished each one.

I would read and reread them over and over, clinging to each word Bob had written. The precious papers were carefully put under my pillow each night, and every day I would write to him. I carefully numbered each letter in case they got out of sequence. I chose my words carefully as I told Bob about the day's events. With the end of each letter, I signed it with a spritz of my favorite perfume. Every letter that Bob received would have my scent on it, bringing him pleasant memories of the wife who so dearly loved and missed him.

All of Bob's love letters were filled with romance, longing, and promise and every letter I received from him had the smell of diesel fuel from the ship. I learned to love that scent. It became Bob's perfume and a signature scent of his own.

LAKESIDE: 2006

Martha found some paper in a drawer in the Gathering Room. She knew she must write a letter. Bob had written her several letters, now it was her turn. She found Kathy and asked her for a pencil. Kathy happily provided what Martha wanted and then went about her morning doing all the chores that needed to be done.

Martha sat at the little desk and wrote for a long time. Kathy checked on her once and found her leaning very close to the paper as she wrote. Kathy knew that whatever she was writing was important to her.

As Kathy was finishing up some dirty dishes that had piled in the sink from the morning cooking session, she glanced around the corner to where Martha was sitting. Martha was carefully folding the piece of paper into a tiny little square. Finally, when Martha finished, she came to Kathy in the kitchen and asked for an envelope. Kathy found one in the desk and handed it to her.

"What were you writing, Martha?" she asked.

"Oh, just a letter to Bob," she replied, "He is in Korea you know."

Kathy nodded her head in agreement and watched as Martha left the Gathering Room. She decided to follow her sweet charge.

Martha quickly scurried to her room with envelope in one hand and letter square in the other. When Kathy arrived at Martha's door to her room, Martha was rubbing deodorant all over the tiny square. She then placed it in her envelope. As Martha turned to leave her room again, Kathy hurried back to the kitchen. Martha came into the kitchen with envelope in hand.

"Where is our big mailbox?" Martha asked as she looked intently around the room.

Kathy knew what Martha was talking about because it would come out of the closet each morning. She told Martha to follow her and lead her to the closet. She opened the door and pointed inside.

Martha pulled the handle down, and popped her letter smartly into the mailbox.

Several days passed after Martha mailed her latest letter to Bob. Martha was enjoying her lunch with the other residents so Kathy snuck away to Martha's room to find all the letters under Martha's mattress. She knew Martha had placed them there, so she lifted the mattress and saw every letter or card that Martha had received over the past few months. Martha often received letters from her grandchildren, daughters and other relatives. She had listened carefully as Kathy read them to her. She always nodded her head in agreement and then carefully folded the card or letter and placed it back in the envelope it came out of. Clearly, she had hidden each one away.

As Kathy pulled each one out, she could smell the deodorant that Martha had spread on them. There were several in the stack that Martha had written and the deodorant had rubbed off onto the others until the whole pile was lightly scented.

Tears welled up in Kathy's eyes upon seeing Martha's painstakingly written work. Kathy knew that Martha could no longer read or write so each note was filled with line after line of scribbles. At the end of each letter, a large bold printed "M" appeared, similar to an "M" a small child would attempt to write. On several of them Kathy could make out the word "kiss" very faintly written in a child's handwriting and then her signature "M." Kathy knew those card and letters were special and were for Bob. Kathy carefully replaced the letters under the mattress and returned to the dining room with a smile across her face thinking of a sweet romance between two young lovers from long ago being relived today.

Martha at 21 years old

Martha's family

The girls of Sleepy Hollow

Martha's wedding Sept. 4, 1946

Young married Martha

Martha and her young daughters

Bob and Martha

Martha and her grown daughters

Martha and her friends at Lakeside

Martha at Lakeside 2006

CHAPTER 14

LAKESIDE, 2006

"THAT WOMAN CAN SING!" CHIMED the caregivers as they lovingly laughed at Martha sitting with the other residents during the Sunday morning Bible study.

Martha would sit for hours if they let her, just singing and singing and singing. She not only liked to sing but also knew every word of every hymn that anyone would mention. She couldn't read anymore, but she could remember the words of the hymns like she was reading them.

She would sing loudly too. She wasn't shy about singing out. Sometimes the other residents would shush Martha because she sang so loudly, but she didn't care, she loved to sing and so that is what she did.

One Sunday, the hymn "Victory in Jesus" was announced. Martha stood up from where she was seated and started singing every word of the old hymn with perfect clarity.

She sang out the words "I heard the old, old story how a savior came from glory, how he gave his life on Calvary to save a wretch like me."

With those perfectly sung words, tears streamed down Martha's face. Doris saw her friend's tears and stood up to hold her hand.

When the hymn concluded, Martha wiped her tears, hugged Doris, and went over to Kathy and thanked her for the revival.

Kathy smiled and thanked Martha for coming.

Watching and listening to the emotions and words pouring from Martha's heart, Kathy was changed that day. She knew that God had placed her here with her residents to teach her something. They were teaching her how to love, to give, and to care.

MARTHA: AUGUST 1949

The air is green pea soup, so thick and stagnant that I wonder how the mosquitoes can fly through it. Hanging above my head, they circle the lights there, unable to get free from the tent's taut ceiling. The only way to move the air around, I decide, is to use a makeshift fan. I join the group of ladies that surround me, fanning myself with the program that was handed to me as I came in this evening.

Bob is still fighting in the Korean War. I pray for his safety every night. I pray for his safety every day.

Bob told me in one of his letters that his oldest friend from Memphis was going to be in town. Bob wanted me to make my meatloaf for Johnny. Of course, I told Bob I would.

I had forgotten Bob's request until the phone rang this afternoon. Stepping out of my comfort zone, I invited him over for dinner, telling Johnny that I would make Bob's favorite for him, meatloaf. It was nice to cook for a man again.

After dinner, he invited me to go with him to this tent revival that is in town for a few days. I had never been to a revival before and looked forward to going. Not because it was a revival, but because it would be good to get out of Glory Ann's house for a couple of hours. Plus, being with Johnny, in a familiar sort of way, makes me feel closer to Bob. It helps to strip away the constant loneliness I feel. Little did I know that God had so much more for me this evening.

As the revival begins, the old preacher stands before the crowd of believers and seekers with his bible in hand. He wears a battered straw hat upon his head and the sweat from his brow puddles on his shirt and the floor like blood dripping from a wound.

His discomfort in the extreme heat doesn't slow the message he sings out to us. With his suspenders pulled tightly at his waist, lifting his pants and showing his white socks below, he speaks of his savior in such a sweet and powerful way that I find myself listening intently. Soon I'm not distracted by his clothes anymore. I find that I want to learn of his God.

The old preacher captures my soul with his words of hope and forgiveness for the lost. I sit spellbound by his words, finally yearning to know this savior he speaks about.

The last hymn of the evening is, "Victory in Jesus". I didn't know the words then. The crowd sings from their hearts as I read them from the hymnal.

> *"I heard an old, old story*
>
> *How a Savior came from Glory*
>
> *How He gave His life on Calvary*
>
> *To save a wretch like me;*
>
> *I heard about his groaning*
>
> *Of His precious blood's atoning,*
>
> *Then, I repented of my sins*
>
> *And won the victory."*

As each word of the hymn is sung, they creep into my soul telling me of the unselfishness of God and His love for me. I feel as if heaven opens up and God is calling my name.

"Martha, come to me" are the sweet words that grip my mind. Tears well in my eyes and slip onto my cheeks and down my face; I know I want to be saved.

Just as the familiar hymn, "The Old Rugged Cross" beckons me to come, the old preacher persuades me forward also.

Walking to the front of the tent tonight, I accept Jesus into my heart. I make that forever decision on this hot, muggy August evening, with Bob's best friend at my side.

LAKESIDE: AUGUST, 2006

Martha put on her oven mitts. There was no hot pan to pull out of the warm oven. It was music time. She always wore the mitts to music time nowadays. She had to. Kathy made sure of that. What a perfect solution to a noisy problem.

If you attended music time, you would quickly understand that Martha loved music. It was her joy. You could see it on her face as she sang, or listened, but she rarely just listened. She wanted to move, to clap, to sing and dance to the music. It made her happy! The problem was her joy was not joyous to the other residents.

When Martha was in the room with the other residents listening music, they couldn't hear it. Martha was too loud! She would clap very loudly, making her hands beet red, and she would stomp her feet. She would sing very loudly most of the time, even if she didn't know the words.

As Martha came in during music time, the others would start moaning and fussing and no one wanted to sit next to her because of the noise she made. With each moan, a little bit of Martha's joy was stolen from her. And with every clap or stomp, joy was taken from the others. Soon, there was no joy left in the room!

So, Kathy came up with the most creative solution. She bought Martha oven mitts, one for each hand. Every day before music time, Martha had to put on her oven mitts. Kathy called them her gloves.

With the oven mitts on, Martha could clap as loudly as she wanted to and she didn't bother the others. Soon, the moans and groans subsided when Martha walked into the room for music time.

Kathy would say, "Now Martha can have her joy without destroying someone else's." She would add: "Sometimes a little muffling of joy goes a long way!"

As a result, Martha was still able to listen and dance herself into a happier place. Singing and making music remained her joy.

MARTHA: WINTER 1939

I stand with the others, absorbing the beautiful music, as the piano player slides her fingers effortlessly across the keys. Oh how I love music!

God has blessed me with a lovely voice. Singing is a talent I didn't have to share with my sister, Glory Ann. I alone have this musical talent. Glory Ann is so good at so many things, but not singing. Secretly, I am glad.

When I hear music, I want to move, to clap, to sing, and to dance to that music. It makes me so happy. Singing in the Glee Club is my joy. As each note progresses, I dance into a happier place. The room, the other singers, and even my circumstances simply drift away from my being as I listen, and create the music escalating me even higher.

CHAPTER 15

LAKESIDE: DECEMBER 2006

THEY WERE YELLOW. SHE KNEW that. They were on her plate. She knew that. But, what to do with them? That was the question her brain seemed to ask. She didn't know.

Lately, Kathy noticed a confused look on Martha's brow, as she would sit down at the table to eat. Kathy would hurry over to her special lady and sit beside her.

She would always say, "Can I help you, Martha?"

Martha would turn to Kathy and say, "No, I can do it," Kathy knew better, so she simply sat down next to her and waited.

Martha's Alzheimer's had gotten to the stage where she was beginning to forget how to eat. She could still chew, but she had no idea what to do with the food on her plate. She would move all the silverware around the plate, basically rearranging them over and over.

After a few minutes of Martha's busy uncertainty, Kathy would pick up Martha's fork and spear a few peaches. She would always ask

Martha if she wanted some peaches, telling her that they were her favorite. Martha always refused the first time Kathy would ask, but knowing that Martha would eventually give in, she didn't give up.

During most meals, Kathy would start with the peaches since she knew Martha would eat them. As Martha finally opened her mouth and tasted them, that same look of familiarity filled her eyes and face. She would pause for a few minutes, remembering.

Kathy wasn't sure what Martha remembered at the moment the peach juice touched her tongue but she knew it triggered a very happy memory for Martha. Once the peaches were on her tongue, Martha would close her mouth and chew them up quickly, like a little child she would make a very satisfied noise. Then, she would smile at Kathy and ask for more. Kathy always made sure Martha had a large portion of peaches on her plate for each meal because sometimes that was all she could get her to eat.

MARTHA: SEPTEMBER 1945

Peach fuzz is stuck to my tongue and the insides of my cheeks. It feels like my tongue has swollen to double its normal size. Licking the fuzz off the peach is something that I am happy to do for the man I had married just three days before.

When we had stopped to buy the basket of fresh peaches from the roadside farmer, Bob didn't tell me that his mother always had to peel the skin off the peach for him. He loved the taste of the peach, but not the skin because of the fuzz. So, that is when I proceed to demonstrate my love for him by licking the entire peach, relieving its skin of the fuzz that grew there. I would do anything for Bob.

Traveling across the country, sitting on the bench seat of the '39 Desoto coupe next to the man of my dreams, nothing could've have made me happier. Even though I can barely speak with a swollen tongue in my mouth, I wouldn't have had it any other way.

We are traveling with a tiny trailer hitched to the car, carefully packed with all our possessions. The wedding gifts, the few pieces of furniture and the clothes, including my wedding dress, are all neatly packed away in boxes and were loaded onto the trailer on the eve of our wedding. Ours is going to be a long honeymoon trip across the country to Bob's next deployment in California. All our worldly possessions are with us. We are in love and together and I could not be any happier. I had dreamed of my wedding day and this honeymoon trip for so long. I can hardly believe it has arrived.

As I ride along with Bob, I gaze down at the petite ring on my left hand. My thoughts drift back to many months before when I had a disturbing conversation with my mother at the kitchen table of the farmhouse, shortly after my engagement.

My mother and I were talking about my upcoming wedding. I told her that Bob and I didn't want a long engagement. We were madly in love and wanted to marry as soon as possible. With Bob being an ensign in the Navy, we were apart so much of the time in our relationship that neither of us wanted to stay apart more than was necessary.

Touching my ring now, I can still feel Mom patting my ring finger as she looked me in the eyes and told me that it was out of the question. She would not hear of me, her younger daughter, getting married before my older sister, Glory Ann. So, unless Bob and I wanted to elope, we had to wait on Glory Ann. I can still hear my mother's words again in my mind, "Glory Ann is the oldest, so Glory Ann is first!"

That was the end of the discussion, and her mind couldn't be changed. I clearly remembered those familiar feelings of being pushed aside once again by my mother, and once again I was waiting on my sister.

So I waited. And waited. And waited. But this time, Bob waited with me.

Finally, the date Glory Ann and Stan picked for their wedding, had arrived. They were married at the local Catholic Church in Sunapee at eleven o'clock by a catholic priest.

Bob and I also set September 4 as our wedding date. We were married at the farmhouse in Sunapee at two o'clock in the afternoon by a protestant minister.

I had followed my mother's wishes. Even though our wedding dates are the same, my older sister did, in fact, get married first. We had a joint reception that afternoon after my wedding. It was in the living room of the farmhouse with several guests in attendance.

Thinking of my beautiful dress, I glance back at the trailer. I secretly wish that I hadn't packed it into that trailer. I wish I had insisted that it go in the car with me. That dress... for this special occasion, at least, I had gotten to pick out the perfect dress for me! It was a antique colored, scoop necked dress with a tight bodice making my small waist even smaller. On my wedding day I felt as beautiful as I had ever felt in my twenty years.

Bob had handwritten me a little note that morning that simply said, "To my beautiful bride, You are the most beautiful bride in the world today. I love you, Your Bob." I had tucked that special note into my purse. It would go in my scrapbook and will be put on the page entitled, "THE happiest day of my life."

Bob and I wanted to get an early start to our honeymoon trip, so we stayed at the farmhouse on our wedding night. The first night was beyond a dream come true for me. Mother had put the best linens on one of the guest beds in the best guest room. She had built a roaring fire in the fireplace and loaded the bed with goose down quilts and blankets. She even allowed us to go to our room early with not one word to us of helping to clean up after the reception. That perfect evening will stay in my heart and mind forever.

As we speed down the highway now we chat about our future together. We talk of Bob's career in the Navy and how we want lots and lots of kids to share our love and life with. Bob wants lots of boys, of course. I dream of a little girl to dress in beautiful clothes that I would make for her.

As our honeymoon trip continues, we grow closer learning about each other more. The days seem to speed by faster as we get closer and closer to our destination. Before we knew it, we were approaching the Rocky Mountains. Bob stops at a small gas station to see that the car's brakes are in perfect shape. He learned years ago from his dad that you never could be too careful. Since we are pulling a trailer, Bob thinks that it best to stop and check everything out. So, we do.

After filling up the car with gas, we start back up the road on our journey. The highway climbs for several thousand feet almost straight up and then we begin the descent. On the other side, the road curves as it comes down the mountainside. It is a windy, curvy road and we have to take it very slowly. Bob is glad he had checked all the brake fluids and the oil in the car.

As we made a sharp turn, I look out the window and over the edge of the road, down the steep embankment. I am afraid of heights and do not enjoy the scenery out my window. As I am about to close my eyes, I notice something out of the corner of my eye. I glance in my rear view mirror only to see the trailer that we are pulling coming up beside us! I can barely get the words out of my mouth when the trailer passes the car on the right hand lane. Bob can't do anything but yell, "OH NO!"

With these words the small silver trailer jumps the curb and flies onto the grass beside the road. Up ahead the road takes another sharp turn to the left, but the trailer doesn't. It proceeds on straight ahead gaining speed, and quickly plummets off the side of the embankment. Bob pulls the car over to the side of the road as fast as he can, slams the car into park and jumps from his seat. I trail behind him. We watch in horror as our little trailer full of all our worldly possessions tumbles end over end down the mountainside, until it finally rests on its side at the bottom of the ravine, landing in a creek. Clothes, broken furniture, packages and bows litter the mountainside above the beat up trailer. I search and finally find my beautiful wedding dress. It is covered in dirt and is lying on the face of a large rock hundreds of feet below us. The tears that well up in my eyes are tears of loss and defeat, but there is a small feeling of hope too.

At that moment I realize that I can handle anything with Bob at my side. The beauty of the mountains that lay before us is overwhelming. Without a word passing between us, Bob puts his tanned arm around my shoulders and together we stand sharing a feeling of awe and humility as we realize that our life together lay before us. Together we stand ready to take it on.

LAKESIDE: SEPTEMBER 2005

The day Marcee had dreaded was here. Today, she was to tour "Memory Care," a part of Lakeside that remained locked and secure and private.

The other residents didn't really know of its existence and they never mingled with the sixteen residents that lived upstairs, behind the locked doors. They never even really saw them except for at the occasional fishing tournament or art show. Even then, only the most functional of the residents from Memory Care would be able to attend. Marcee had never been there and frankly didn't want to go.

Martha had lived downstairs at Lakeside for four months. It couldn't be said that she was happy for those four months. She kept thinking and telling her daughter that she would be leaving at any time. In fact, she kept packing and repacking her suitcase that Marcee had left in the closet.

As the months progressed, she seemed to be more and more bored, displaced, and unhappy. She stopped drinking her Diet Pepsi. That was a big shift in character for her. She loved Diet Pepsi. For as long as Marcee could remember Martha had had a Diet Pepsi in her hand or on the table next to her, no matter what she was doing. She usually drank five or six of them in a day. During the first few months at Lakeside, Marcee had had to constantly refill her little refrigerator in Martha's apartment. Nothing else could fit in that little refrigerator besides her beloved Pepsi.

Not only did she drink her diet pepsi, but she also gave them away to others that would stroll by her apartment door. The dining room did not serve soft drinks, but since Martha liked them so much, the caregivers always brought one down for her during mealtimes.

There were three things Martha enjoyed at Lakeside: she loved the musical groups that would come to sing, she loved the preacher that preached on Sunday mornings (he was a singing preacher, the best kind according to Martha), and she enjoyed the food in the dining room. She had a very hardy appetite. Besides those three things though, Martha didn't seem as if she enjoyed Lakeside. Marcee wanted her mom to be happy but it seemed that she couldn't find that for her.

One day, Gordon approached Marcee as she entered the front doors to come visit with her mom. He told her that he had concerns about Martha. She had joined the walking club. Not that joining the club was a bad idea, but when the walking club got tired and quit after 30 minutes or so, Martha would keep going. She walked around and around the facility all day long, every day. He said that she kept going because she was looking for Bob. She told Gordon that she knew Bob was there but couldn't find him.

While Gordon was telling Marcee about the walking club, she thought of her visits. Lately during every visit now Martha would ask her, "Where is your father? I can't find him." So Marcee knew that Gordon was voicing the same worries she herself had but didn't want to admit. Gordon told her that because of Martha's decline, he felt like she needed more care. She wasn't happy and she was bored.

He told Marcee that he had started allowing her mom to go up to "Memory Care" during the day. He told her that Kathy, the head caregiver upstairs, would come down and get Martha in the morning after breakfast and bring her back downstairs at suppertime, so she could eat in the dining room. Gordon called it Martha's day care. Marcee was astonished at his choice of words. She did not want to think of her mother getting worse, much less that she was getting so bad that she needed "Memory Care." However, Gordon stayed firm in his opinion. It was the place that Martha had to go. She could no longer remain downstairs. She was not happy and they were worried now that she might try to leave to find Bob or her daughters. "It is apparent that Martha also needs more structure," he stated decisively. Memory Care could provide that for her. She couldn't read, write, or create much on her own anymore, so she was bored. Upstairs in "Memory Care," the caregivers plan every minute of the residents' day. There would be no time to wander and be bored.

Thus, Marcee had finally arrived at that most dreaded day. She made her way upstairs following Gordon and listened to him tell her about what they were about to see.

"These residents need lots of care. There is one caregiver to every three residents. Memory Care residents need to be told what to do and how to do it, when to sleep, eat, and dress. The caregivers upstairs are our most highly trained and most compassionate of all the caregivers we hire. If a resident needs help eating, bathing or dressing, that is provided. Today you will meet Kathy. She is in charge of the other caregivers up here."

Marcee followed Gordon to the double metal doors, down the hall from the elevator. He entered them by using a code to unlock the doors. When inside, he made sure the doors were secure. *Would Mom know she was locked in?* Marcee wondered.

As they turned to walk down the hall, they were greeted by a woman carrying a doll. She didn't seem to see them. She was staring at the doll she carried while moving her lips speaking softly to the doll as she stroked its bald head. Gordon stopped to admire Gertrude's "baby" and commented on how big her baby had gotten. Gertrude smiled and continued walking. Marcee knew that her mother would never believe that a doll was a real baby. She just wasn't ready for this place!

As they approached a large windowed room, several ladies were sitting at a table making a craft. There was glue, paint and cotton balls, and a huge mess all over the table. Two women in green scrubs were assisting the three older women as they concentrated on the project at hand.

A gentleman was sitting in front of the T.V. watching the Lawrence Welk Show. Another woman was holding hands with the lady sitting next to her and they seemed to be deep in conversation. One younger woman was helping an older woman out to the patio where many more residents sat and laughed as they were throwing a large colorful beach ball around the circle of chairs. Then Marcee noticed a beautiful flower garden planted on the hillside by the patio.

The flowers could be seen from the big sitting room. Artwork that looked to be created by first graders adorned the walls, bringing the colors of the flowers from outside, inside. She gazed at the artwork thinking how sweet that a local children's class hung their work on the walls for the residents to enjoy. Then she noticed Gertrude's name printed in an elementary handwriting on the bottom corner of a paper. The artwork she made was a finger-painting of nothing she could recognize.

Gordon was giving her "the five-cent tour" as he called it. Marcee tried to pay attention to what he was saying but she kept getting distracted by the residents and their activities. There was so much activity around her. They all were busy doing something. They smiled and laughed. Most of them seemed happy enough. A few sat alone or seemed to walk around aimlessly, but most were engaged and active.

Marcee still wasn't sure. To her, Martha's condition wasn't nearly as advanced as these people. *Could she possibly need to be here doing finger painting and simple crafts?* Marcee wondered, feeling completely unready for the possibility.

Gordon took her to the kitchen door. She looked around the large room and there was a caregiver in her scrubs helping two ladies make cookies at the far counter with their backs to the door. They all were wearing aprons and one of the ladies was wearing a tall chef hat. They laughed and then giggled like little girls playing together or having fun with their mother.

Marcee smiled then for the first time that morning. She and Gordon stood watching the three for a few minutes, then Gordon cleared his throat. As he did so, the caregiver turned around and smiled as she wiped her gooey hands on her apron. She approached them. The other two women didn't seem to notice and kept making cookies.

"Hi Kathy," Gordon said, "This is Marcee, Martha's oldest daughter."

Marcee smiled and shook her extended hand.

"It is so nice to meet you," Kathy said and turned to the ladies. "Martha," she said, "Look who is here!"

To Marcee's utmost surprise, the woman with the chef's hat turned around, revealing her mother. She knew the look on her face was that of surprise and shock.

"Oh Hi Marcee," Martha happily says, like it was perfectly natural for her to see her daughter standing there. "Doris and I are making chocolate chip cookies. When they are done, you can have some, okay?"

She smiled again and turned back around to finish making dough balls with Doris.

For the first time in months, Marcee saw her mom's smile. She actually was smiling and laughing and having fun. About that time Doris took a piece of dough and put it on Martha's nose.

They both squealed and giggled and Martha called to Kathy, "Kathy, look at what Doris has done! Doris is so funny!" She then turns towards Kathy to show Kathy her nose.

Kathy turns from the two visitors and laughs along with the older women as she wipes the dough from Martha's nose with her apron.

"You girls are so silly!" Kathy chuckles and the three women continued laughing as they put the cookies on the cookie sheet.

Marcee sits down, almost in shock, realizing suddenly that her mom did belong in Memory Care. It was exactly what her mother needed.

The next week, Martha was moved upstairs. It was like a band of elves magically and mysteriously transported everything from her room downstairs to a similar room upstairs. Every stick of furniture, every photograph on the wall, every piece of clothing and even the glass of water sitting on her nightstand all were moved and placed exactly in the same spot they had occupied downstairs. The move was done while Martha was busy planting flowers in the garden one morning. The funny thing was…Martha never even noticed.

As Kathy was pulling the covers up over Martha's shoulders on that first night, she asked if Martha wanted some water.

"Yes, I think I will," Martha says as she reaches to her nightstand for the glass that is always there.

Kathy was glad Martha had moved in upstairs. There was something special about her and Kathy was looking forward to getting to know her better. Tonight, Kathy decided that it would be Martha's turn to have her temples rubbed.

Each night, Kathy spent a few minutes with several of the residents, tucking them in and talking about their day in an attempt to help them relax before bedtime. She had learned early on that the scent of lavender was relaxing. So each evening, she chose three or four of the residents and rubbed their temples with a little bit of lavender lotion as they lay in bed with their eyes closed. She decided that since Martha was new, she needed it tonight.

As Kathy begins to rub Martha's temples with the lotion, Martha begins to doze off.

Just as Kathy is about to leave Martha whispers, "It was a good day today."

Kathy smiles and softly whispers back, "Yes, it was a great day, Martha. Go to sleep now and I will see you in the morning."

With those words she gently kisses Martha on the forehead. Before Kathy can leave the room, Martha is breathing heavily, already dreaming of Bob.

CHAPTER 16

MARTHA: SPRING 1943

I FINGER THE NEW SKIRT I wear as I drift over to the window. It is a cool New York day, just the way I like it. Looking below, I see the doorman opening a car door for some passengers. A couple slides from the car seat and onto the sidewalk. They are in love. It is plain to see. I know how it feels to be in love.

Last weekend, Bob had come to see me. He had brought a special ring for me. He asked me to marry him. I'd said yes.

Today, he rode the train up from Memphis. He wants me to make the trip back to Memphis with him to meet his family. I am so nervous! Meeting Bob's family is a bit overwhelming, but I know Bob will make it easy for me.

As I look into the distance, I see a man in a uniform, running up the sidewalk. It is Bob! I run down the flight of stairs, not waiting for the elevator. I am at the front door before Reggie could open it. As I turn the corner, I run into his arms. The feel of his strong arms around my small waist makes me relax and melt all at the same time, as always. That feeling never seems to fade no matter how many times he holds me.

"Well," Bob sings out in his southern drawl. "Are you packed and ready to go?"

"Of course I am," I reply.

Holding each other tightly, we head back up to the apartment. As the elevator cage door slams shut, the elevator slowly rises. Bob reaches over and kisses me gently.

"How's my girl?" he asks softly.

Looking down I whisper back, "I'm fine but I missed you."

Many hours later, our train pulls into the Memphis station. I peer out the dirty window. Bob's head is pushed against mine as we look together. Soon, he spots his family waving. He franticly waves back, jumps up and pulls me with him out of the seat. We are the first to exit the train. His mother, father and sister are all there to greet us. Bob hugs each as he continues to hold tightly to my hand. I stand on the platform looking down. Bobby's mother is the first to speak and welcomes me to Memphis. The train ride had been a long one and I was exhausted.

Bobby's mother says, "You must be tired, dear. Come and let's head to the car." She pulls me along with her as we leave the platform.

Bob chats happily with his father and sister as we all head towards the car. As the five of us turn to leave the station, the train blows its whistle loudly.

LAKESIDE: JANUARY 2006

"Is that the train whistle?" Martha asks as she looks toward the hill above the patio. "Are we going to Memphis?" is her next question. She listens for a long time.

Bob rides the train when comes to visit sometimes. Maybe he's riding the train today, she thinks. The residents sit on the patio when the weather is nice. There are comfortable chairs and sometimes they will play with a ball. There is a fence surrounding the patio, but you can see and hear past it.

The fence holds them in, but their memories carry them out. As they sit quietly listening, the sounds of train whistles, airplane engines, dogs barking, children playing, and familiar voices ring out and call to them. Martha sits and listens for a long time as her mind drifts to happy places and happier thoughts...

MARTHA: SPRING, 1942

"Glitz, glamour, love and life." Four exciting words spring to my mind. "Words...expressions of feelings....and eyes into the soul. There is so much power in a word." I meditate on that thought as I feel the pulsating rhythm of the wheels against the tracks. I love reading those words, reflecting on them, and expressing them, especially in a painting, but sometimes I hate feeling them. There is so much power in a word.

These four fantastic words linger in my mind now as I peer eagerly out the dirty window of the train car. I see my reflection in the window and I am smiling. It is a big smile, one that I can't hope to contain. My new life is awaiting me in the exciting city of New York.

"Welcome to New York City," I read on the worn sign beside the tracks. More words. These five words have captured my imagination often these last six months. There it is, appearing magically in front of me, The Big Apple. The tall buildings that had lingered in the far away distance of my mind occupy my landscape now and I realize that my own imagination hadn't done the reality justice. As the buildings grow, so does my nervous excitement. I have never been so far from home before. I have never taken on such an adventure. I have never felt so free.

Daddy took me to the train station in New London this morning. It was a long drive from the farm. We had plenty of time to chat about the summer. We talked of the campers, the kittens that will be born, and the repairs we will need, meaningless topics really but simple things that memories are made of.

Mother had packed a lunch for us and we nibbled on it as we talked. Fixing food is what she does. It's a tangible way she likes to show love. Mother was too busy to accompany us to the station. She told me that the end of the summer was one of the worst times for me to be leaving the farm. She complained all morning about having to stay behind to do all her own chores and now mine. I wonder now if her words were meant to hurt or if Mother said them to cover up her true feelings.

Daddy hadn't wanted to talk of my leaving Sunapee to pursue my dream, and neither did I. So we didn't. I know Daddy will miss me terribly. When I told him about the letter of acceptance to Pratt Art Institute six months ago, he smiled with a smile so dear to me. It was a smile of pride and love all wrapped together, one that I will never forget.

Although Daddy is a man of few words, I can read him better than anyone. I knew by the look on his face that he will always be proud of me and he wants me to be happy. If going to New York City will make me happy, then I know he wants me to go, even if he doesn't want me to go. I will miss him the most. We have a bond unlike any one else in the family. Daddy routinely whispers in my ear at night as I go to bed that he loves me more than all the stars in the universe and I always say the same thing in response to him, "No, I love you more, Daddy!"

Mother rarely utters the word "love" to anyone, not even Glory Ann. Perhaps she and Daddy tell each other that they love each another in private, but never in front of us. I think it's very sad. I know when I get married love will be the main topic of conversation. Sometimes though through her actions, like with today's lunch, I know in my heart that Mother loves me but I still always long to hear it.

This morning as I was leaving Sleepy Hollow for New York, Mother barely spoke to me. She busied herself doing odds and ends around the kitchen, nothing important, just business to fill the time.

Words…I needed and wanted words, but they didn't come, not from Mother. As if she was making some sort of love gesture, Mother had pulled a bill from her apron and stuffed it into my hand as I walked out the door with Daddy. With the stuffing came a slight pat on the hand and then she turned to wash another dish in the sink. Not a word was spoken or a hug given.

"Martha's pipe dream" is what Mother constantly exclaimed when the subject of Pratt Art Institute had been brought up previously. I always take to heart everything that Mother says to me, but this time was different. I just can't accept what Mother wants for me. I am following my dream and there is nothing Mother can do about it.

Sitting on the train car now, I finger the bill in my pocket. I pull it out and crumple it tightly in my fist. I know I will need money, and for a short second I contemplate stuffing it into my purse, but then out of defiance or maybe pride, I suddenly throw the money on the train car floor and kick it with the tip of my pointed shoe. It slides across the slick floor and rests under the bench opposite me, out of view. A sense of freedom and satisfaction comes over me as I once again peer into the distant scene of the city waiting for me.

JAMES: SPRING 1942

I slowly drive the distance back to the farm after leaving Martha at the train. I stare blankly out the front window of my truck as it bounces along the streets. I don't see the view. I only see my beautiful, wide-eyed beauty that I so dearly love. I allow the tears to flow as my mind takes in all of her sweetness. I am filled with pride and hope for my sweet, quiet Martha and the life that lay before her.

EDITH: SPRING 1942

I remain at the little kitchen window idling longer than I want, staring out onto the grass, but not seeing it really. I allow a single tear to fall and one thought to pass through my mind of my youngest daughter. I know I will miss my reckless, disheveled, and talented daughter. I shake my head then to dislodge the warmth growing in my heart, let my breath escape my lungs, and continue with the chores.

"This little window needs a good cleaning," I think as I grab the cloth and begin wiping the smudges away on the glass.

Martha, Spring 1942

I sit on the train, peering out the train window, realizing that I am riding this train into my dream. Tears well in my eyes as the joy and dream became real.

The clanking of the metal wheels on the iron tracks catches my attention and draws me out of my thoughts as the tempo slows somewhat. I am aware of my beating heart now. It beats in rhythm with the sound of the wheels on the tracks.

As the train continues to slow, I see that we are approaching a station. Glory Ann is to meet me at a station. As the conductor walks by my seat, I listen for the station name.

"Claremont Street Station," he yells loudly enough for all to hear. I pull the slip of paper from my bag and look at the words.

"No," I think, "This is not my station."

The train slows to a stop and many of the passengers get up to leave. I stay in my seat.

As soon as all the standing people got off the train, it starts up once again following the conductors booming voice yelling "All aboard."

I take another deep breath and relax again as the train speeds up to its traveling speed. I am not allowed to rest for long, when once again the train starts to slow.

Again, the conductor walks through the train car shouting, "Wilshire St. We are approaching Wilshire St. Station."

My heart jumps in my chest as I recognized the name that is written on the scrap of paper that I still hold tightly in my fist. I look then out the smudged window for my big sister.

The train approaches the covered boardwalk near the tracks and I know it wouldn't be long now before we stop and I will be in New York City with all its flashing lights, rushing people, and bustling activity.

I look even closer out the window but don't see my sister still. As the train pulls slowly into the station, I gather my bags and my suitcase. I place my hat on my head and stand to walk the short distance to the car door. I move up the aisle with the others, barely containing my excitement. It is difficult getting all of my bags down the aisle and out the door, but I finally manage and step down from the train.

When my foot touches the platform, the train whistle blows loudly and I almost lose my wavering balance. I knew it hadn't been a good idea to wear my new platform shoes.

I grab the post beside me as I drop my suitcase. My gloved hands are sweating by this time, but I was glad for them as the bag handles dig into my hands making blisters on my palms.

Mother had insisted that I wear my "Sunday best" for the trip to the city. It was not worth a last minute argument with her so I did as she insisted. Now I wished I had worn my sweater and slacks along with my comfortable flat shoes like I had wanted. I would have been able to move more freely in this crowd.

Scooting away from the tracks with the crowd surrounding me, I am moved by the pressing and pushing bodies. The crowd encompasses me like a wall, keeping me upright and moving in the direction that I assume I should be headed. As the crowd of New Yorkers finally starts to thin out, I stop to collect myself.

Glo is nowhere to be seen. I continue to the station building with all of my bags. I stand again, looking into the crowd for the familiar face of my sister. All I can see are strangers hurrying along their way.

I had written to Glory Ann several weeks ago to tell her what time my train would arrive and ask if she could pick me up. She had responded quickly saying, "Of course I will be there."

So I wait. I finally put my suitcase against a pole and sit on it to give my feet a much-needed rest. I watch the people and enjoy imagining where they are going and why they are at the train station.

I imagine that the young couple kissing near the open train door is saying a long good-bye, both of them dreading the moment their kiss has to end. An elderly man rushes past me holding the hand of a child appearing to be his granddaughter. They both have a look of excitement and adventure as they hop onto the waiting train. A group of military men gallop along in front of me, cavorting with each other as they laugh, joke, and then look in my direction. As they glance my way, I lower my gaze and turn around to avoid their eyes.

Looking down the platform, I see a group of beautiful young women walking in a row. There are three of them. Each woman is swinging her handbag and tossing her hair with her free hand. It is as if they are in a movie, walking in slow motion towards me. I study their painted faces and curled hair as they draw nearer.

Oh how beautiful, worldly, and glamorous they are, I think. They each hold their chin high and seem to have a practiced wiggle in their stride. These women are obviously successful business women that are meeting a business partner at the station, or perhaps they are models going to an audition across town. *That is probably it*, I decide.

As the group passes in front of me, I can't take my eyes off of them. One of the women looks in my direction as I sit leaning against the post. The woman slows, turns and then approaches me.

"Martha?!" the woman screams.

I cup my hand over my eyes to shield them from the sun and before I can say anything the woman says, "It's me, Glory Ann. Stand up here and give your big sis a hug! How was your trip?"

All of these words tumble out in one very fast minute and I am shocked. How much older and more sophisticated she looks, I think to myself. I stand to embrace the sister I hadn't seen in a year.

Glory Ann's red lips, blonde curls, seamed stockings, and high heels are all I can see. The other two women join us then and hug me as well.

They are quickly introduced to me as Celeste and Chloe, Glory Ann's roommates and best friends. They each grab one of my bags and we walk off down the platform arm in arm, all talking about nothing and everything and New York and glitz, glamour, love and life.

I look to my left and then to my right at the women and smile. My smile is a big one, one that I can't hope to contain.

CHAPTER 17

LAKESIDE: AUGUST, 2005

ON THE LAST EVENING BEFORE Martha was to go to Lakeside, her daughters had one last task to complete. Gordon had told them that before their Mom came to Lakeside they needed to replace all her jewelry with costume jewelry. He said that many of the residents would lose items they brought with them. They tended to misplace and hide things, and he hated for any expensive jewelry to be lost to the family forever.

Following his instructions, Martha's daughters tried to replace her favorite pieces with costume ones. One necklace that Martha wore constantly was a small gold heart on a delicate gold chain. It was difficult finding a copy of this specially made necklace that Bob had given to her on their anniversary, but the sisters did find one similar. They told her that the necklace needed to be cleaned, and then they replaced it with the one they had found.

Martha's diamond engagement ring was the toughest to change. It was white gold and very tiny. She still wore it every day with the tiny wedding band that accompanied it. One evening the ladies told their mother that they needed to clean her diamond. She had worn that special ring for the past fifty five years, rarely taking it off.

Even though they tried, that ring remained tightly clinging to her finger without budging. Susan decided to get a bar of soap and rubbed it over the ring and exposed finger. With great difficulty and many groans from Martha, it finally slid off. After cleaning her ring, her family replaced her diamond with a store bought cubic zirconia ring that resembled the much-loved ring. Martha never noticed the difference.

GLORY ANN: WINTER 1944

I hurry down the busy sidewalk securely holding my blowing scarf around my hair so as to not mess up my new do. My lips are freshly painted with a new red lipstick that just arrived in the Five and Dime. I can't run very fast in the high heels I wear daily to my job at Hudnutt's Department Store. I am late, and I know how important this is to Bobby.

Over the past few weeks, Bob and I had become good friends. Bob was one of those boys that everyone liked He had been the captain of his high school football team. He was even voted Mr. Southside High. Bob was very handsome and outgoing. All the girls thought he was a catch.

A few weeks ago, Bobby had asked me to meet him at Grover's Jewelry Shop around the corner from my apartment.

As I see Bob, I quickly slow to a stroll, pulling the scarf down around my shoulders. I smile, hugging Bob and planting a big ruby red kiss on his cheek. He looks so handsome in his uniform. It had been weeks since I had seen him. He had ridden the train up from Norfolk today to meet me. He told me he had chosen two rings and couldn't decide on the perfect one for his Martha, so he had asked me to meet him to help make the decision.

As I walk into the shop with him, a tiny hint of jealousy rises within me. I fight these feelings, trying to be glad that I am able to help Bob with this task. Upon gazing longingly at the two rings he had chosen, I immediately choose the dainty diamond that matches my sister's small delicate hands. Bob agrees that the diamond is perfect. I pick up the ring and try to put it on, but it was only a size four, way too small for my long fingers. I smile as Bob pulls out the money he had saved and pays the jeweler for his purchase. Placing the precious box into his pocket, we walk arm in arm back to the apartment to meet Marty. She will be surprised and I can't wait to see her face when she sees her engagement ring!

CHAPTER 18

LAKESIDE: MAY 2006

FISHING AT LAKESIDE WAS AN activity that all the residents enjoyed. Martha had gone fishing with Bob many times on his boat, but she rarely, if ever, fished herself. Regardless, today she suddenly decided she was going to catch the "big one." So, with pole in hand and a hat on her head, she headed off with the other residents to the dock on the lake next to Lakeside.

A family of geese sat on the bank basking in the sun. Martha needed help getting her fishing pole ready and baiting the hook. As they were working on the line, Martha wandered off towards the lake. Perhaps she was getting too close to some eggs or baby geese but suddenly she was running with a large goose biting her on the bottom over and over as she ran towards the others screaming. "Help me" she yelled, "Help me, Mother!"

MARTHA: SUMMER 1937

I love going to Sleepy Hollow. It is our summer home. Our family named it Sleepy Hollow because the sleepy property actually nested quietly in the hollow of two small mountains.

"Summer home" is not exactly accurate since it is the only home our family owns. We live at Sleepy Hollow in the summer because my mother and father run a guesthouse here. The rest of the year, we share a small apartment on the campus of Colby Junior College where Mom and Dad work.

Mother is the cook for the female students at Colby while Daddy does all the maintenance for the school. Mother and Daddy had scraped together every extra bit of money they had to buy the farm, hoping to be able to make additional money in the summer. They planned to open the farm as a guesthouse and summer camp for girls.

Every May we arrive at Sleepy Hollow after the college closes for the summer. We spruce up the old homestead for our guests. Walls have to be painted, rugs beaten, and the linens have to be carefully washed and hung to dry. I love the few weeks that we work together with no guests around.

We all work. Daddy fixes whatever had been broken over the winter and cleans up the yard. He also has to chop all the firewood that will be needed for the summer. New Hampshire can still have some very chilly evenings and mornings in the early and late summer so there is much to chop. I loved to play around the wood as a young girl, back when the pile reached over my head.

Mother worried about all she had to do in the house and in the cottages, cleaning them to perfection, making them ready for the guests. Glory Ann and I each had lots of chores to complete too.

My favorite time of all is in the evenings when we come together again as a family. After dinner and a hard day's work, Daddy listens to the radio and sings along with all his favorite tunes. I sit in his lap and listen. The fireplace is warm and Daddy's voice is so melodious that often I fall asleep in his arms. Whether I do or not, he always carries me up the stairs and puts me to bed in one of the guest rooms. The featherbeds are so soft and warm and the quilts are piled so high that I can bundle up in the layers and sink deeply into the bed like a "little bug in a rug" as Daddy lovingly says to me.

In the early morning, as the frost creeps around the edges of the glass in the old panes and the breath from my lips flows out like the smoke from the chimney, I can smell Mother's breakfast cooking on the old pot-bellied stove. The aroma of fresh eggs and bacon sizzling in the pan rouse me from my dreams and make me eager to face the day of work again.

The big red barn with the neatly painted geometric Hex Sign sits at an angle behind the house with a large grassy field between them.

Way back on the birch tree line at the edge of our property, the guest cottages sit neatly in a row. When all the guests arrive for the summer, they will occupy the guest rooms in the house and the cottages, leaving the barn loft as space for my sister and me to sleep. Mom and Dad stay in the room off the kitchen.

I cherish these first days of the summer embracing the comfort and warmth of the house and closeness of my family.

As Glory Ann and I grow older, it is now our job to be the maids for Sleepy Hollow, cleaning all the rooms and cottages. We also have to plan activities for the children. We plan crafts and games and take the children swimming at Lake Sunapee, which is a short distance from our property. I especially like to watch the geese and her babies in the early summer as they swim so gracefully across the lake. We take with us picnic lunches that our mother carefully prepares for each family as we walk the guests to and from the lake each day.

In the evenings when our work is done, Glo and I creep up to our large loft room above the barn. Sometimes we peer through the cracks in the loft floor watching the activities going on in the barn below. Many evenings we organize dances in the barn for the guests and then will spy on them from above. Occasionally, a guest slips away to the barn to meet another guest secretly, not aware of us spying from above. On most of those occasions, we hear things that we shouldn't.

For two weeks during the summer, my sister and I hold a girls camp. Wealthy girls from Boston and other big cities nearby come and spend part of every summer with us. This is my least favorite part of summer, but it is Mother's favorite. The camp brings in the much-needed money that she and Dad need to keep Sleepy Hollow running.

I hate having to deal with the spoiled, selfish, and uppity little girls that come. Glo and I work harder these two weeks than any other time in the summer.

Towards the end of the camp, we have had enough of the campers and simply stop trying. Isabella and Nancy are the worst of all the campers. They think they own the place. Slavery ended a long time ago, but you wouldn't know it by the way these two act. Glo and I hate them.

Isabella would waltz into a cabin like a queen parading before her people, her head held high and nose held higher! Oh how I hated the look or even the thought of her. Every summer she and Nancy would come to Sleepy Hollow Girls Camp and every summer I would loathe them. Of course, I had to treat them nicely on the outside, as my mother had made quite clear, but my mother couldn't control my mind. I was free to think anything I wanted and I most certainly did!

These girls are rich, very rich, and they let everyone know it! When they started coming to the camp, I was fifteen years old. They were twelve and already had their airs about them. Their clothes are the best money can buy and they had so many! Sometimes when all the girls were down at the lake or eating dinner, I would sneak into their cottage, making sure that Mother didn't see. I would look through their closets and envy all their clothes.

The fabrics were so rich and when I ran my hands over their garments, I could feel the money beneath my fingertips. As I carefully touched the material, I would pull it up to my nose and smell it too, taking a long whiff of the lovely fabric. I love the smell of expensive fabric. Each summer their wardrobe would be different and each summer I longed for a time in my life when I might buy expensive fabric and sew beautiful clothing. I would sneak back out of the cabin after admiring their clothes and hate them even more.

It was a night like any other. All the girls were in their cottages for the evening. Suddenly shrill, screaming voices break the silence of the cool, quiet evening. Mother is at the sink, washing up the dinner dishes, tired after a long and busy day. Suddenly she is jolted from her tranquility by the uninvited noise. She throws the wet dishcloth to the floor and gallops as fast as she can across the field to reach the loud commotion.

Flinging open the screened cottage door, she finds two of the camp girls, Isabella and Nancy, rolling on the wide-planked floor. Each girl has a handful of the other's hair gripped tightly in their fists. Biting and kicking, they fight with fury.

Mother quickly scans the room and finds Glory Ann and me standing in the shadows smirking as we watch the little brats fight it out. Grabbing both campers by the scruffs of their skinny little necks, Mother quickly stops the fight. Then, looking at us with extreme distaste, she proceeds to sit the girls down and takes control of the ridiculous situation while we look on. As both girls momentarily relax, they start crying in unison, each attempting to appear more upset than the other. Then the bickering starts once again between them.

Our mother has no patience for such silliness and demands that they stop their bickering. She helps the two girls make amends. Eyes wide with interest, Glory Ann and I watch as our usually impatient mother tolerantly solves a menial problem between the campers.

As the tension passes and the girls' problem is resolved, Mother shifts her gaze to us once again. We know from the coldness of her glare that we are the ones in trouble. Smiles now wiped clean from our faces, we wait for Mother and her lashing words.

Mother hugs each camper lovingly, whispers good-night to them and then motions for us to follow her out. Glory Ann and I follow her out the cottage door. Isabella and Nancy sit on the bed together watching us scornfully as we trudge out to face our fate. They stick out their tongues at us and shake their curly heads in our direction, mocking us as we step out the door.

Once outside, far away from the little cottage and the eager ears of the campers, Mother turns to us and proceeds to yell at us with the same intensity Isabella and Nancy had used screeching at each other just moments before, as if she had somehow swallowed all of their rage. Her tongue spews out words that sting. Words that neither of us feel we truly deserve.

According to her, the campers are our responsibility, and she is furious with us for allowing the fight to happen. These two girls are money, as good as cold, hard cash. Money we need. Money we can't afford to lose. There is no excuse for our lack of supervision or management of the situation, she tells us. Then our mother spins away as her last biting words are seared forever in my memory: "You are irresponsible, unappreciative, and above all inconsiderate girls, and I am NOT proud of you!"

Trying to make my mother proud and trying to forget her biting words from the night before, I attempt to do as my mother insists, trying harder to concentrate on the campers .

One of the chores given to me during the summer, was hair washing. I was designated the hair washer for the guests while Glory Ann was the hair fixer. I didn't mind it because every guest paid five cents for a hair washing and Mother allowed me to keep that money.

I would set up a wash basin on an old wooden table hauled down from the barn and place it in front of a painted kitchen chair. I would choose a spot outside where the sun bathed the grass so it would be comfortable and warm for the guests. I had to haul buckets of water from the lake or the faucet and the campers would line up single file to wait for their turn. My favorite part of the job was getting to use the special soap Mom made particularly for the occasion.

Mother would make the soap every winter in our little apartment kitchen. She would use the best scents she could find and spend hours boiling the lavender or rose petals or whatever scent she could find to make the soap. She was known all around Lake Sunapee for her handiwork. The tiny apartment kitchen would smell so heavenly that I would sit outside the room, smelling and dreaming and smelling and reading and smelling and sleeping. The fragrance was so wonderful that it carried me to far-off places that I never dreamed I would see. So every summer when I washed the heads of the ladies and girls, I was reminded of the faraway places I had imagined as the soap had boiled on the stove.

The bar of soap would become smaller and smaller with each head washed, and I would get more and more excited. I knew that when the bar got too small to use I could get another, and the little sliver of soap remaining would then slide into my pocket. At the end of the hair washing sessions, I would take the little saved pieces of fragrance and hide them in a bag in a secret place in the barn. I then would long for the end of summer so the guests would leave and I would be allowed to use up the small pieces I had collected. Without Mother knowing it, as I cleaned the bathrooms I would sometimes sneak a piece that was left behind and save it in that same sack in the barn.

At the end of the summer I knew I would get to smell like our wealthy guests, if just for a short time. I used the delicate smelling soap sparingly in my hair and on my body. I tried to make it last as long as possible into the fall or even the winter if I was lucky.

MARTHA: SPRING 1940

I danced from the house to the barn. It is a beautiful spring day on the farm. No guests had arrived yet and I was to take the basket of daffodils mother had given me over to one of the cottages. How could I not dance as I go, carrying such beautiful flowers? As I pass the barn, I am drawn inside. My secret cache of paints were there and my inner passions were tugging at my heart. On such a gorgeous day I just could not refuse them; I need to paint. I gravitate towards my makeshift art studio hoping to capture the beauty of the flowers in my hands, knowing all the while that I am disobeying my mother so I hurry. I jump the wooden steps two at a time as I ascend into the loft.

Hidden under a loose floorboard are my paints and a brush. I pull all the tubes out and quickly choose the few that would make the colors I need to capture the bouquet. I mix on an old board and within minutes have the perfect hues. I pull some paper from a dresser drawer in the corner. It is paper we use with the children during the summer when they come to camp here. I borrow pieces from time to time.

I place the basket on the ledge of the window, the sunlight streams in from the window illuminating the delicate daffodils. I can not imagine a more inviting image for an artist. The painting comes together quickly and I am very pleased.

As I sit admiring my completed work, I hear Mother come slamming out of the screen door shouting for me. I had been so involved in my painting that I hadn't realized how much time had passed. I know that my mother does not share my passion for art and will be furious with the time I wasted up in the barn.

I quickly throw the tubes of paint back underneath the floor and hide my still wet painting under the bed. Mother arrives at the barn just as I am coming down the steps from the loft.

"What have you been doing?" she asks sternly looking as if she already knows the answer to her question. She looks at the flower basket in my hands and shouts , "I gave you that job two hours ago!"

I lower my head and keep quiet. It seems best not to respond.

"Martha, what have you been doing?" she demands again.

Finally, I speak up but will not lift my head. "I have been painting this basket of flowers, Mother," I honestly reply.

"What!" Mother screams at the top of her voice.

"You have been dawdling around with that waste of time! We

barely have the time to get the chores done around here, and you are up in the barn painting?? I have had it with you! Now go and put that basket in the cottage, come right back to the house and go to your room. You will have no dinner tonight, young lady."

With those harsh words, she stomps back to the house to complete her daily work. I slowly walk to the cottage to finish my own job. I place the basket on the table in the cottage and start to cry.

Mother does not understand me! She will never understand my passions! I think to myself not willing to share my thoughts with my mother., *I love to dance, to paint, to sing, to act and Mother cannot see it. She only sees what I can't do.*

As I dry my tears and head to the house defeated, I can see Mother watching me as I make my way across the field. I hear her voice in my head say once again, "Life is hard, you have to learn a skill, a trade. You can't spend your time dancing or singing or painting. What good would any of those things do you? Times were tough and we must be tough. After all, that is how Daddy and I have survived, hard work and toughness." As I slip in the door, Mother turns her back to me and I pass by without a word or even a nod.

Mother served her dinner to Daddy and Glory Ann that night. My seat remained empty. I knew Daddy was on my side, but I could tell he didn't want to argue with Mother. She had become hard and callused in the last several years and there was no changing her mind. I knew it and he knew it, but he still came to visit me later that evening and brought me a small helping of pot roast.

LAKESIDE: SPRING 2006

Martha stood at the table with her paintbrush in hand. The fish were staring at her from the paper. She was wondering why they were not orange. Goldfish are supposed to be orange. She didn't have any orange, only purple and green. She slammed the brush down and sat down.

"What is wrong, Martha?" asked Kathy.

"Fish are orange!" she screamed.

"Okay then, I will get you some orange paint," Kathy quietly replied.

Martha pouted as Kathy strode across the room through the other painters to get the orange paint.

Doris eyed Martha's work and said, "It's pretty."

Martha scowled at her, crossed her arms, and turned her back to her best friend.

When the orange paint arrived Martha knew what to do. She grabbed it from the teacher and began to paint. She painted and painted, getting orange on the floor, her chin, and Doris. When she finished she handed Kathy her brush and smiled.

"Good Job, Martha. You are a good painter," Kathy said, "You have talent and you worked hard."

Martha's painting entitled "Orange Fish" was sold for forty dollars, the most that day at the Arts and Crafts Sale held yearly by the residents to raise money for Alzheimer's disease research.

CHAPTER 19

LAKESIDE: DECEMBER 2006

IT WAS TIME TO GET up. The sun was streaming in on her as Martha's eyes focused on the forest animals gazing at her through her window. There, just outside, was the familiar band: the deer, rabbit, the squirrel, a raccoon she had not met before, and of course a few birds flittering about to complete the group. Her animal friends came to see her quite often now. She liked them. They were the best company. They seemed to smile at her in their own animal kind of way.

Moose was good company too. He was always there with her for as long as she could remember. He loved his doggie treats and would sit up at any moment to get one. Bob sure did love Moose too. She reached for her sweet dog as he sat in the chair. He was right where she left him the night before. What a pretty dog he was! He had the smoothest black and white fur. Martha patted Moose right behind his ears in the special place that he liked.

As she got out of bed, putting Moose down, she looked in her chair for her clothes. Kathy hadn't come to wake her this morning so she would get herself ready for school today. She searched for her white jean pants and found them folded neatly on the stool at the foot of her bed. She had a hard time these days zippering and buttoning but finally they were on.

She grabbed her pink underwear from her underwear drawer and put them on. They seemed a bit snug this morning. Maybe that extra cookie for dessert last night was just too much.

Martha grabbed the bright green blouse that was hanging neatly in her closet and finished getting dressed. As she searched for her favorite sneakers and socks, she saw that Moose was on the floor. He was just lying there quietly. She hated to wake him, so she left him there though she knew that her bed was his favorite place to sleep.

Once her shoes and socks were on, she left her room to head to breakfast down the hall. As she made her way to the dining room, she saw Doris. Doris ran over to walk with her friend. Doris grabbed Martha's hand as they walked together chatting about the forest animals.

Kathy was setting the tables and turned to see Martha and Doris entering the dining room. At the sight of Martha, Kathy stopped what she was doing and walked over to the women.

"Hi girls," she cheerfully greeted.

"Oh hi Kathy" Martha and Doris sang in perfect harmony.

Kathy could hardly keep from laughing out loud at the site of Martha wearing her underwear on the outside of her pants.

"I see you got yourself dressed this morning, didn't you, Martha?"

Standing as tall as a proud little girl could stand, Martha pushed out her chest and proudly proclaimed, "Yes I did!"

"Well…you did a very good job young lady" was Kathy's less than truthful reply.

The women shuffled together into the room and Kathy took Doris to her place at the table. She whispered a secret into Martha's ear and off the two of them went, leaving the dining room.

Martha was giggling as Kathy led her down the hall to her room. She tried very hard to find her name by her door. It was just so hard to find the right room, but since Kathy was with her it seemed easier.

"Look for the M," Kathy directed. "M for Martha" she said.

The women finally found the "M" and opened the door. Kathy went into Martha's room and shut the door behind them.

"Those are pretty pink underpants you have on today," she told Martha.

"I like them too. Mother got them for me," Martha replied.

Kathy helped Martha sit down on the bed as she pulled the tight underwear off of her jean-clad legs. Martha started giggling when saw her pink underwear lying on the floor as if reminded of an old joke...

MARTHA: SPRING, 1933

Smoke billows from the smoke stack of the 4:55 as it sits at the station waiting for its passengers to board. The commotion on the platform is infused with the sounds of yelling voices, wheels screeching, and babies crying. Glory Ann and I hurry beside our mother as she rushes towards the train.

Mother looks very appropriate wearing her freshly ironed though slightly worn sable brown cotton dress with the big white collar for traveling. Her hat sits at the perfect angle to compliment her determined face. Her gloved hands hold our smaller bare ones as we scurry along the wooden platform. Her stylish platform heels don't in any way slow our pace.

Approaching the train, Mother stops too abruptly, releasing her grip of our hands. She begins to frantically search for the tickets she had just purchased at the window.

The conductor takes his place by the train's metal steps with a glance at his pocket watch and yells "All aboard" in a loud and urgent tone.

We have seen that look of resolve on our Mother's face before and don't dare utter a sound. Although I know exactly the place of the tickets in Mother's purse, I remain silent. She opens the clasp of the crocodile purse hanging from her arm and recklessly searches within.

As she pulls the hidden tickets from her bag, I sigh and take a breath of relief. Mother is standing with her legs slightly ajar, bracing as she looks. Her pretty, pink panties slip from their place upon her waist. In all the hustle and the bustle, the elastic has suddenly broken, sliding them gently down her legs. Just as she proceeds to pull the tickets from her purse, the pretty pink panties fall quietly to the floor. Glory Ann and I spy the pink pile that had fallen at our mother's feet and try to restrain our laughter. Mother doesn't seem to take notice, and with a carefree attitude, simply steps from her panties and leaves them lying there on the platform floor. As the train leaves the station and the travelers occupy their seats, the pretty, pink panties remain unnoticed in a heap.

LAKESIDE: DECEMBER 2006

Martha was still giggling when Kathy asked, "Did you see your forest friends this morning, Martha?"

"Oh yes, I did" Martha replied quickly in her sweet little girl voice, as she glanced out her window.

"That's wonderful!" Kathy said, "They sure do like to see you in the mornings, don't they?"

Now that the underpants situation was taken care of she had to find Martha's bra. It was not in her drawer, nor on her chair. In the closet, Kathy saw the open suitcase, with many of Martha's dresser clothes stuffed into it. There amongst the other clothes was the elusive bra. Kathy made a mental note to ask Marcee to take the suitcase home. It was time. Martha still had moments when she knew that she was not at home, and in those moments when her brain was remembering she would pack her bag to leave. It was time for the suitcase to find its way to Marcee's closet and out of Martha's.

With the bra and pretty green shirt on, Kathy reached for Martha to give her a hug and said, "Good…we are ready now. Your green blouse looks so pretty with your dark eyes–just a perfect color for you! You did such a good job getting dressed this morning. I am very proud of you."

When she stepped forward to give Martha the hug, she stepped on the stuffed dog that Martha's grandchildren had brought.

"Oh my," Kathy squealed. "I almost stepped on Moose! What was he doing on the floor?" She picked up the gift from the ground and handed him to Martha. Martha kissed Moose on the head and gently placed him on her bed by her pillow.

"There," she smiled, "He is back on the bed now. I love Moose, you know," whispered Martha.

"He loves you too, Martha, almost as much as I do." replied the sweet guardian.

CHAPTER 20

MARTHA: WINTER 1940

IT IS HARD TO BELIEVE the evening has finally come. It is the night of the annual Winter Carnival Dance. I watch as Glory Ann slides confidently across the middle of the dance floor making her way to the opposite side of the room. Every male eye is glued to her every move. She purposely glances towards the closest group of young men as she bats her long, blonde lashes and flicks her blonde curls with her gloved hand. Every step is with purpose and confidence.

Her lovely new dress swirls around her long, stockinged legs demanding their attention. I continue to watch my older sister from the shadows. I timidly lean against the wall trying to fade into the woodwork behind me. My dark eyes, wide with yearning, are soaking in every detail. I know Glory Ann is everyone's favorite. I know, too, that my place is in the background, behind her. After all, Glory Ann had resumed Shirley's role as the eldest child the day Shirley died, leaving a place for her, but there was still no place for me.

Earlier that afternoon, my sister and I had readied for the big dance together. Mother had taken us to McCall's dress shop to buy new dresses for the evening. Glory Ann was cranky and complained that it was awfully late to be looking for the dress, with only 3 hours left until the dance. It had been a very busy day for Mom at Colby College where an unexpected ironing job had to be completed before she could leave. I was just excited that I was going to be able to pick out a new dress.

Most times, when there was an event to go to, Glory Ann got the new outfit and I wore one of my sister's older dresses, but this time it was going to be different. I was excited to be able to pick a color that looked best on me. With my dark eyes and long, auburn, hair, the colors that my fair, blonde sister would pick just did not flatter me as they did her.

As the three of us reached our destination, Glory Ann began her task. She paraded around the store with pomp and circumstance, displaying every dress that she could try, including the lovely green one from New York that was on the mannequin in the window. She climbed onto the pedestal in the middle of the shop, and spun around and around, admiring the gentle flow of the hem and how it shifted around her legs. It was lovely on her. The green fabric of the gown pulled the color from her eyes.

Earlier, Mother had told us that we could spend only thirty dollars together; that was all she had. I found my special dress immediately. Both Mother and Glory Ann had commented that it was pretty, but only after looking at the price. I alone admired my reflection in the mirror, noting the perfect fit, style and color of the dress on my tiny frame. My dark eyes and hair were complimented by the subtle hues of the blue collar. Upon finding that perfect dress I sat patiently waiting for my sister to finish.

Mother scurried about my big sister fixing the ruffles and bows, admiring her figure in each one. This process was like everything they did. I would make my choice without fanfare and comment while Glory Ann demanded the attention of everyone in the room. Sadly, this shopping trip began just as all of their outings did and ended the same as well.

As Glory Ann's choices narrowed, the expensive green gown captured the attention of the saleslady. Being excellent at her job, she commented that Glory Ann was as beautiful as a model in Paris wearing the gown, and there was no price that could buy that. Mother and Glory Ann succumbed to every word the woman uttered until they too became convinced that it was so. Mother happily pulled the thirty dollars from her purse, placing it on the counter with a smile. The saleslady wrote the receipt as she thanked the two for their purchase.

Watching the circumstances unfold, I felt a familiar disappointment and sadness in my heart. Without notice from the others, I quietly replaced my gown on the rack and left the store. Mother helped the saleslady clean up the discarded gowns, not thinking of me.

As her task was complete, she then looked for me. She found me outside on the storefront bench. Sitting beside me, she tried to fix the damage. She didn't realize that it was too late. The damage was done. That damage had been done for a long time. She assured me that everything would be just fine, and that I could wear one of Glory Ann's gowns. She would find the perfect one for me hanging in the small closet at home. I don't know why I had allowed myself to get excited.

Why did I think it would be different this time?

LAKESIDE: MAY 2006

Today was dress up day in Memory Care. Each resident was given a manicure and a makeup session with the caregivers. Kathy always did the hair. It was a fun day for everyone.

Martha was standing next to the opened closet door trying to decide which gown to put on for the afternoon tea party. Families had donated beautiful prom dresses from their past to Lakeside so the women could dress up. There were many beautiful gowns in the closet to choose from. It was so hard to make a decision.

Martha wanted to choose the bright red beaded gown, but she wasn't sure. Her nails had just been painted and she chose red for them so why not choose the red dress as well? She looked around the room for Glory Ann and her mother, but they weren't there. She pulled the special red dress from the closet, and her mother filled her mind once again. Would her mother allow her to get the red dress? Would things be different this time?

Looking at the beautiful dress, she held it to her body. She could see that she would look lovely in it, almost like a model from Paris. She turned then and told Kathy that she wanted to wear it. Kathy smiled and told Martha that she could wear whichever dress she wanted. Martha smiled. She knew then that she didn't have to wear one of the dresses in Glory Ann's closet tonight.

"I want to wear this red dress, Kathy," Martha said with certainty.

EDITH, SUMMER 1973

I hop into my red Karmann Ghia. I had to save and save for a long time to get the little convertible of my dreams, but I did it and I was even able to pick out the color. Red, my favorite color! Oh how I love to hop in it and scoot about town with everyone watching as I fly by. I glance at my bleached blond hair, dark glasses, and brightly colored scarf that flutters about my neck in the mirror.

"Just perfect" is my only thought. I love it when the wind blows my blonde curls and my scarf every which way as I drive too fast down the road.

A smile slips from my lips as I realize just how hard it had been and how far I had come in my seventy-four years. I have my pension from Colby College. I have my social security check from the government. I can make ends meet. After seventy-four years of making ends meet, I definitely know how to do it.

After having four husbands, I know how to do that too, but the one thing I love even better than men is clothes. The louder the style and color, the better! The bigger the statement I can make, the better. Since money has always been tight, I wear my clothes over and over, year after year, buying a new pair of shoes or a scarf to enhance each one.

I especially love special occasions, so naturally, I have a "special occasion" section in my closet. This section is home to a blue church dress with a matching hat, my flowing, white brocaded "wedding dress" (which isn't really a wedding dress at all), and my black conservative funeral dress and veil. I see no point in buying a new dress for each Sunday or each wedding or for each funeral.

With each new husband, I put on my "wedding dress," and with the passing of each of the men I loved and married I would wear the same black conservative funeral dress and veil. After all, I can make ends meet this way.

After the fourth marriage and subsequent funeral, I almost gave those two dresses away, thinking surely at age seventy-four I was done with weddings and even funerals. Even though I took excellent care of each of the garments, they were beginning to get worn and frayed.

It was more of a surprise to me than to those who knew me when Ray came along shortly after my seventy-first birthday. Everyone told me I looked beautiful on our wedding day in my "wedding dress." Unfortunately for him, after a year of marriage, I buried Ray while wearing my black conservative funeral dress and veil. Still, that would not be the last time I would wear the much-used white brocaded "wedding dress."

I have no intention of wearing my somber funeral dress to my own burial. I plan to go out it style. My guests will look in at me in my coffin that day and note how pretty and appropriate I look wearing the brightly colored scarf around my neck and new white sandals upon my feet. The lovely brocaded, white dress will look stunning on me, a perfect outfit for a hot summer day. My lips will be painted a bright red, along with my nails and even my toes. Upon my face, the hint of a small, satisfied smile wouldn't go unnoticed. I intend for everyone to leave saying that I went out in style.

CHAPTER 21

LAKESIDE: MAY 2006

MARCEE CAME TO SEE HER mom on Mother's Day. She brought a bunch of pretty spring flowers in a vase and a package from Susan. Leslie had sent a present last week and Martha loved it. She carried the stuffed bear around with her for an entire week.

Martha didn't know that Leslie, Susan or Marcee were her daughters and she didn't understand Mother's Day, so the day was more for them than for her.

She smiled when Marcee arrived with the flowers and placed them on her nightstand. She opened Susan's gift like a small child at Christmas. The pajamas fit well and they were soft and comfortable. Martha said she had to put them on right then and wore them for the rest of the afternoon.

As they were sitting in the dining room ready to eat, Martha turned to her daughter and said, "Mother, can I have some ice cream after dinner?" Being accustomed to being called "Mother" sometimes, Marcee just answered her with a "yes, sweetheart".

Edith: Summer 1959

It was one of those days where the long, straight highway had a transparent wavy film hovering just above it. The heat from the pavement rose above radiating into the open windows of the station wagon. The only relief was the breeze that blew into the windows as the old car sped along. When the car stopped at a traffic light, the heat was stifling. Martha was singing "We Ain't Got a Barrel of Money" while Bob hummed along. They seemed happy with plenty of room in the front seat of the car.

I, on the other hand sit crowded in the backseat with my two young granddaughters on either side. Their damp, sticky, little bodies are pressing against mine. The dog is panting loudly behind my neck. His long pink tongue hangs limply from his drooling mouth. An occasional drip hits me on my bare shoulder. Perhaps the pink halter-top was not the one I should have worn on this summer day, but my plaid peddle-pushers with a hint of pink look perfect with the top.

As I ride along with my daughter's family, I am beginning to question my decision to accompany them on their vacation this summer. As the hours drag on and the sweat beads on my forehead and under my arms, I decide that I can't handle this heat anymore.

Tapping Martha on her shoulder, I interrupt her conversation and ask Bob to stop at the next gas station.

"Let's stop and get some ice cream, Bob. It is SO HOT and I cannot go any farther until I get refreshed,".

Not needing gas yet, Bob starts to argue with me but then says,

" Okay, Edith. We can stop."

As we roll up to the gas station, I hop from the car, accidentally smash my equally hasty granddaughters on the way. I stand and straighten myself, pushing at my hair and wiping the sweat from my face. Glancing at myself in the car mirror, I decide I am presentable and head in the direction of the bathrooms, ice cream having completely left my mind. The only thought on my mind now is cooling off and getting out of the very crowded car.

I know that the bathrooms are always located around the corner from the front door at gas stations so I head around the back of the building as the attendant washes the front windshield. The longer I walk the more urgent my need becomes, so I hurry even faster. I fling open the bathroom door, where darkness greets me.

With my pants already unbuttoned, and without a thought or a look, I quickly pull my clinging pants down and spin on my heel to sit on the toilet. Suddenly, one scream and then another is echoed inside the small room. I don't know if I screamed first or the man sitting there doing his business, but nonetheless, neither of us are happy. I am sure everyone outside hears the loud screams and probably looks towards the direction of the commotion.

Annoyed, I scurry from around the corner, buttoning my pants and smoothing my hair, whilst heading towards the back seat. I don't take the time to look around to see if anyone has figured out what all the commotion is about.

Sitting once again in my assigned spot, I pull my bright red lipstick and mirror from my bag and retouch my lips. I see Bob's smiling face in the rear view mirror but know he won't say a word.

The incident around the corner of the gas station was never talked about as Edith knew it wouldn't.

LAKESIDE: APRIL 2006

Visitors always came to the Gathering Room. The large, sunny room was decorated with comfortable furniture and a large television that sat in the corner. Every chair had a view of the patio and the colorful flowers outside. Handmade, seasonal decorations hung on the walls and from the ceiling, each one bearing a resident's name. The carpeted floor warmed the space, making it like home.

Martha and Doris sat together eagerly awaiting today's guests. Without much delay, the local Brownie troop filtered into the room, arriving with youth and smiles and pets. Each girl walked in carrying a different one.

A little dark haired girl smiled at Martha and approached her chair. She held the baby kitten close to her chest. The girl's smile softened as Martha asked about her charge.

"What is her name?" Martha quietly asked as she watched the kitten yawn.

"It is Sally," answered the girl with the look of a proud parent upon her face.

As Martha's old and wrinkled hand reached for the small and soft kitten in the Gathering Room that day, her aging and diseased brain reached into its deep and wide recesses to find a buried memory of a long ago day…

MARTHA: FALL 1933

"They will be fine." Mother tells me in her most stoic voice, as big tears roll down my face. "Wait until spring and you will see," she says, trying to reassure me as I stroke the small kitten in my arms.

Our beloved farmhouse is all closed down for the winter. It is time for us to leave Sleepy Hollow and head to New London. All the guests have come and gone for the year. We can't afford a season without an income, so we must return to the college.

I worry about the barn cats during those cold winter days and nights in New Hampshire. Next year we will return to the farm in the spring to ready the house for the new guests and I hope that just like last spring, the cats will return to the barn, just like Mother promises.

The momma cats carry their babies in their mouths to the farmhouse from the barn then. Every spring, Mother prepares the bottom drawer of the chest next to the wood stove in the kitchen for the new litter. The babies will grow up there in the soft, warm blankets until they are too big and then out they will go to the barn.

Mother is like those Momma cats, tough when they have to be, yet soft and loving when they need to be. I quietly observe her behavior and slowly begin to notice her softer side.

CHAPTER 22

MARTHA: WINTER 1935

I WAKE UP AND IT IS very dark in my room. I don't like being in the dark. It scares me. I get up out of my bed to find Glory Ann.

I leave my room and walk slowly down the dimly lit hall. I can't quite remember where Glory Ann's room is. I know it is down the hall, but where? I finally find her door, open and look inside. There I see my big sister sound asleep in her bed. She has a night-light on in case I need to find her. Glory Ann always looks after me and I know she left it on so I could find her.

I pull down the sheet and blanket ever so gently and crawl under the covers next to my big sister. Happy to be with her, I fall sound asleep dreaming of the upcoming camping trip.

LAKESIDE: OCTOBER 2006

At two o'clock. every morning, Patrice would go to check on each resident. She started at one end of the hall and proceeded down the hall checking each room.

Martha's room was the second one she checked. She was surprised to find an empty bed. She called for Martha, in case she was somewhere else in the apartment. She wasn't.

Patrice alerted the other caregivers and they started their search. The doors at the end of that floor were locked and there was a keypad entry, so they knew Martha couldn't have gotten off of the floor. She was there somewhere.

The caregivers went into each room without finding her. Doris' room was the last one on the hall. Doris was Martha's best friend. Maybe she was there.

As they opened the door, and peered into the dimly lit room, they found Martha cuddled up with Doris, her arm around her best friend's waist. The caregivers smiled to each other at the site of the two women cuddled together. They were glad Martha had found her Glory Ann for that evening. They gently escorted Martha to her own bed and gently patted her back until she fell back to sleep in her own bed in her own room.

LAKESIDE: THE NEXT DAY...

The next day's forecast threatened rain, so when Marcee arrived she knew that the caregivers would have the residents out on the back patio while they could, before the rain set in. The residents loved to be outside.

Today was the perfect day for it. The clouds billowed in the sky overhead, the birds sang, and the breeze blew slightly from the north bringing with it a cool breath of air. Marcee saw her mom as she opened the patio door.

"Hi Martha," she says.

Martha was sitting in a striped patio chair next to Doris. She was looking over the chain link fence into the clearing, with a slight smile on her face.

Marcee quietly approached her. "Hi," she says again.

Martha turns and looks at her with a puzzled look for a moment, as the present seeps back into her mind. Then a huge smile fills her eyes and face as she recognizes the young woman she loved so much.

She reaches out for her daughter's hand, squeezes it, and squeales, "Oh, Hi Glory Ann!" in her most excited voice. "Does Mom know you are here?" she cries enthusiastically.

Marcee says "yes, she does" as she sits down as Glory Ann.

During most of her visits now, Marcee was Glory Ann. Occasionally, she was "Mom", but never her real name, Marcee, Martha's eldest daughter. Marcee belonged to a faded memory of a life that had slipped away. After all, Martha was a twelve-year-old schoolgirl. She had no husband or children of her own, of course, only her older sister, Glory Ann, her Mother, and her Daddy. She loved them. She adored Glory Ann.

She had Doris, her best friend, and the other girls and teachers at her school. This was the past-life world Martha lived in now. It was a very pleasant world and she was very happy. In fact, she was the happiest Marcee had ever seen her.

They sat together, a daughter and a mother, both longing for the same thing, their mother. One was able to escape, to find hers. The other was bound by reality, slowly losing hers. Both were content and at peace. They sat, without talking, simply holding hands, staring at the clouds...only

MARTHA'S MIND READIES FOR AN ADVENTURE...

"I look above my head. There suspended above me are giant marshmallows in the sky. So soft and white that I want to reach up and squeeze each one and take a bite. The puffy clouds hanging above me hold back any rain that might form there. The wind is blowing ever so slightly from the north bringing a cool breeze to the day. The sounds of birds singing make the unfolding scene surrounding me seem like a scripted play.

I decide to go find Doris. It's a perfect day to go camping. As plans to camp out race inside my mind, I see my best friend coloring a picture at a table.

"Come with me, Doris," I whisper to her. "We are going on great adventure!" I tell her excitedly.

Doris nods her head in agreement.

Hand in hand, we run out the door. Together we climb the fence into freedom. It isn't a hard climb for us. We love to climb! Running as fast as our legs will carry us through the tall wavy grass, we giggle and laugh without a care in the world. We are ready for our adventure and nothing is going to stop us today.

Soon we find the ideal spot, and make ready for our day. The clearing in the wood is a perfect spot, complete with a fire pit that is all set up. The rounded stones are laid neatly in a circle and the wood is already placed in a neat heap upon the dirt floor of the clearing. The green tent is there too, just the right size for two twelve-year-old girls.

There in the woods Doris and I spy a mother deer and her baby peering around a bush, with their eyes big with wonder. We pretend not to see them, hoping they will come closer. A nosy rabbit family that lives nearby stops to sniff at us, wiggling their noses ever so slightly.

"Camping is such fun when you go with your best friend" I say.

From a distance I hear Mother calling to me and realize our camping trip must wait a bit longer. It is almost time for dinner.

"I'm coming Mother!" Martha calls, breaking the silence and yelling as if she were far away.

"What?" Marcee says to her mother, turning to look at her.

Seeing the happiness in her mother's eyes, Marcee smiles realizing her mother is somewhere far away. She puts her arm around Martha as she cuddles closer. Once again their roles are reversed, but they find comfort from each other's embrace.

CHAPTER 23

LAKESIDE: JANUARY 2007

HER EYES ARE CLOSED. HER body still. They hadn't had any response from her now for the last twelve hours.

My tummy is hurting and I am very tired. I can hear people talking around me, but I am too tired to open my eyes. My forest creatures will be waiting for me to say "Good morning." Where are they?

Doris's voice in my ear interrupts my thoughts. She is asking me to come play with her on the back patio. I love my best friend and I love to play, but my stomach hurts more now. I just want it to stop. I know I can't go play with Doris today.

I remember Daddy telling me to pray in my time of need, so I talk to God as I look out my window. I ask him to take away this terrible pain. He doesn't talk back, but I don't mind.

I can still hear people talking to me, but they aren't very loud. They want to know what I am looking at out the window. I don't want to talk to them because I am trying to concentrate on the man outside.

I remain quiet, watching. I watch him for a long time. He is standing beside a tree, looking at me. He starts to come closer and smiles at me. He has a very nice smile, one that says, "I am your friend." He reaches out his arms to me and says, "Come to me my child."

Then I know. As I obey His gentle voice, the window fades, along with the voices. As I follow him further…I feel free. I feel safe. I know joy! I know love.

The nurse had said that it wouldn't be long now. Marcee had hoped that Susan would be there in time. The plane that carried her from California wouldn't arrive until that afternoon.

Marcee sat on Martha's bed, gently holding her hand as Leslie was talking to her softly. They had coffee and food, Gordon saw to that. They had all the comforts one could need, but they didn't feel comforted.

People were in and out that morning checking on Martha. Most came to talk to her, some simply to hold her hand. Kathy had been with them late into the night, and again since early that morning. She loved Martha almost as much as her daughters did. Her eyes were swollen as she brought Doris in to see her best friend for the last time.

Doris looked at Martha and smiled. She came slowly over to the side of the bed and looked really close at Martha's face. She placed her hand on Martha's cheek, and rubbed the face she loved. The ladies wondered if she was aware of what was happening to her friend. They could not restrain their tears from falling as Doris slowly walked over to the chair where Moose was sitting, picked him up gently, and cradled him in her arms. She lovingly placed Moose, the stuffed dog, next to Martha's hand. Doris knew Martha loved Moose and would want him right next to her. Doris patted Moose as she whispered in Martha's ear. Leslie and Marcee looked at each other, knowing that Doris couldn't talk. She was mumbling something important into Martha's ear. When Doris said what she wanted to say, she turned as a single tear slid down her cheek.

The heaving of Marcee's chest and her tear soaked cheeks seemed to surprise Doris as Marcee gave her a long hug. The tenderness of Doris' smile at that moment was a gift that God gave Martha's daughter in her moment of need. Without a word spoken between them, Kathy slowly walked Doris from the room. Their emotions were cascading, and Marcee and Leslie were exhausted.

It was a beautiful January morning; the meadow and trees outside the window were filled with life. Though the leaves were absent, the trees provided warmth and shelter from the cold for the animals that lived there. The scene was a beautiful one, one that Martha had loved every morning as she awoke.

As her daughters admired the beauty outside the window, suddenly and without warning Martha opened her eyes wide. Those familiar eyes were searching and seeking. Her once limp body straightened as she looked fervently out her window. Leslie and Marcee too, jumped to attention, watching this miracle unfold before them. Martha could not and would not take her eyes from the scene out the window. Leslie asked her who she saw. Finally, after minutes that seemed like hours, she told them.

In a weak little girl voice, she whispered, "It is Jesus". Then she repeated her words again, "It is Jesus."

Her daughters looked at each other with a common knowledge. Martha was going. They knew with certainty that at that moment, their mother was being drawn to a familiar, spell-binding love that called to her…and her Heavenly Father was looking down on His daughter, His beautiful, wide-eyed beauty and smiling, giving her a peace that passed all understanding.

With a total feeling of awe and overwhelming humility, they whispered to their mother that it was all right and for her to go to Jesus. As the tears welled in their eyes, a delightful recognition filled hers….

As the voices around me become faint, the total recognition of truth encompasses my being. I am no longer the four-year old of my mind, but once again have all the wisdom and knowledge of the eighty–two year old child of God that I am. The realization of God's words fill my soul as I am drawn towards my Savior.

> *When I was a child, I talked like a child, I thought like a child, I reasoned like a child. When I became a woman, I put childish ways behind me. Now we see but a poor reflection as in a mirror: then we shall see face to face. Now I know in part: then I shall know fully even as I am fully known. And now these three remain: faith, hope and love. But the greatest of these is love.*
>
> **1 Corinthians 13: 11-13**

On that day, with the clear memory of all eighty-two years of her life, Martha left her earthly home and made her way to her heavenly home with Jesus.

CHAPTER 24

JANUARY 3, 2007

MARTHA WAS DRESSED IN HER favorite creased, white jeans, and striped nautical shirt. Her bobbed hair fixed the way she liked it. She wore her bleached tennis shoes on her small feet. Her daughters nearly giggled when they saw her outfitted in her boating clothes as if boarding the boat ready for a day at sea with Bob, but they all knew that it was the perfect outfit for her. The stillness of her body and the eerie quiet brought their experiences of the last two days into the forefronts of their minds. It was over, but none of them could say it. Their mom's two-year battle with Alzheimer's was finally over. As they turned to leave they felt an unsatisfying relief.

A numb feeling came over each of them as they readied to leave their mom for the last time. Clumsily, and with a sudden sense of urgency, they gathered their coats, scarves, and purses and proceeded to the door.

Shutting the door behind them jarred their thoughts to the

realization that they had just closed that chapter in their lives forever. That chapter that had consumed them for over two years was finally over. With every step they took they felt the walls closing in on them, making them desperate to reach the front doors. Each of them was eager to grab a breath of fresh air. They picked up their pace down the darkening hallway. Hearing hushed whispers from behind closed doors interrupted their thoughts, tearing them away. They were all together in that moment of time, but each felt very alone.

As they turned to enter the lobby and saw the front doors ahead of them, they were anxious for some fresh air. The three sisters struggled to get there needing some relief. They stepped into the dark, cool night and stood breathing in the fresh cool air. It was a cleansing of sorts, allowing them to expel some of the sadness grasping at their hearts. Refreshed for the moment, they continued on their way towards the parked car down the block.

Passing by the lit storefronts along the sidewalk, the colorful windows beckoned to them to notice what lay behind the glass. Marcee slowed as the other two walk quickly down the sidewalk leaving her behind. Gazing through the window, her mind wandered as she noticed the beautiful clothes in the latest styles displayed on the mannequin in front of her. The young woman had obviously just walked into a room decorated for a party. Other mannequins dressed in their party attire greeted her with unopened packages adorned with beautiful, brightly-colored ribbons. Marcee imagined it to be a surprise party for the young woman. The woman seemed happy, with a bright red smile upon her painted face. The others too wore painted smiles and held out their gifts for her to take.

The happy scene took Marcee away for a few moments, escaping the reality she was trying to forget, but then she heard her sisters yelling from down the block.

"Open the car door!" they shouted as she turned to hurry to where her sisters waited, her grief rising again. Getting inside out of the cold weather, she slid into the driver's seat and started the car.

Leslie scooted into the back seat and pushed aside a box. It was wrapped in white paper, tied with a fluffy silver bow that covered the box completely.

"What a beautiful wedding present" she thought as she placed it to the side with great care. *Marcee must be going to a wedding soon,* she thought. Leslie sat in silence, smiling in the back, allowing herself to be distracted with weddings and gifts and parties, trying to ease her sorrow.

The car ride from the funeral home was a silent one. Each daughter was attempting to deal with their mother's death in her own way and each prayed that comfort would come to them magically through the silence and reflection of a life they knew was full of depression and sadness.

As each of them grasped for snippets of good times they had with their mother or a fond memory they shared with her, comfort was nowhere to be found. In those few minutes, they each attempted to rationalize to themselves that their mother's life mattered. But did it? They could not outwardly express the questions in their minds as the car sped along. Did her life mean anything? Was her life a positive influence? Was she ever happy? It was a fruitless venture that left them sadder and more withdrawn than before.

Upon arriving at Marcee's house, they were greeted with darkness and a coldness that reflected their mood. They each desperately needed the warmth and security of an inviting place at that moment, a place that would wrap around them like the warm arms of a loved one. They desperately fought against the knowledge that the peace and comfort they sought could not be found within. Seeing the darkness of the house left them more lonely and numb than before.

They robotically stepped out of the car and walked to the front porch. Susan ascended the stairs first and noticed a large, nondescript package blocking her path as she reached for the door. Her mind wandered to what the contents of such a package would be, thinking of the many unexpected packages she happily had received from family and friends over the years. That momentary thought was comforting and she relished in it for those few minutes. But being enveloped in darkness she had kicked it unintentionally, thus returning her to the reality of the evening. She bent down and picked it up. Each sister then took note of the box, but continued in their methodical manner to get in out of the cold air that gripped their bodies and their souls. Their minds searched outward for the protection they craved inward as they stepped through the door.

Attempting to combat the darkness, they each searched for a lamp and the light to fill the empty space. Shedding their coats, scarves and gloves, each sister noticed that the temperature inside was not much different from out. Feeling the unusual chill, Marcee went to the thermostat in the hall in an attempt to erase the cold. After turning up the furnace she walked back through the den. She saw Susan carrying the package that was at the door and watched her place it on the floor. The light and comfort seemed to elude the sisters and they each remained reflective and alone.

The evening meal was prepared and though none of them were hungry, they each deliberately ate, trying to fill the emptiness with food. Insignificant conversation filled the silences. All the while the sisters tried to dissect the burden within their hearts. Dinner ended and the three headed to the back porch.

As Leslie joined her two sisters on the patio, she carried the still unopened package with her and placed it on the stones beside the fire pit. Forgetting the package, she wrapped herself loosely in the blanket hanging from her chair. Each of the girls was quietly nestled in their own Adirondack chair as the fire was lit and began to crackle.

As the fire struggled to warm the sisters, they began to pull their blankets more tightly around their shoulders to cocoon themselves, not allowing the unwanted cold night air to enter or the cold of their hearts to surface.

The only sounds heard were their heavy sighs and the only thing seen was their warm breath billowing from their lips as it mixed with the smoke and cold air, creating a fog of sorts surrounding the group. Unsuccessfully trying to shake the cold feeling, they simultaneously slid their chairs closer to the fire in order to get some relief.

The warmth emanating from the fire provided some relief from the bitterness, so they slowly released the tight grip of their blankets and allowed the warmth to envelope them. As each of them stretched their tired feet forward to rest on the edge of the fire pit, they began to feel a bit more relaxed and slightly warmer. Two of the sisters were able to get quite close to the fire, but Leslie was unable to move her chair. There was something blocking her chair.

Noticing then the plainly wrapped box beneath her chair, she pulled it out and handed it to Marcee.

She said, "Here, aren't you going to open this?"

"Yes," Marcee replied, "Hand it to me,"

Leslie handed the package to her sister. This allowed Leslie then the freedom to also move her chair closer to the fire.

Taking the package from her sister, Marcee placed the box next to her in the seat and said, "You know girls, we have to come up with a eulogy for Mom for her funeral tomorrow. What are we going to say?"

With a sigh at the unwanted chore, they nodded their heads in agreement. The girls started to discuss the problem facing them. They began to feel the warmth and glow of the fire; they dropped the blankets from their shoulders, exposing their arms to the warmth allowing the penetration of the heat to warm their core.

Susan replied to her sister's question, "At most funerals people talk about the deceased and the wonderful accomplishments of their life… and all of their accolades…and as her daughters, how we admire her. What would we say about Mom?"

Leslie was quick to answer and stopped mid-sentence as she realized the question was more difficult than she thought.

Marcee also answered, "Well…that's easy….we can say…," before she too stopped.

Silence once again commanded the scene as the sisters tried to come up with something they could say. Their list was short: she made balanced meals for the family, she was devoted to their father, she looked younger than her years, and she kept them well dressed and clean. Then there was a long pause.

"Is that it?" Marcee asked. "That is so sad."

Once again the sisters retreated into their minds, reflecting on their conversation and realizing together that it was the best they could come up with. Disappointed, the sisters sat back in their chairs trying to think of something to add. None of them could. Letting her mind drift, Marcee picked up the plain box.

Susan asked, "Who is it from?"

"There is no return address" Marcee replied.

"Well, whom is it addressed to?" Leslie asked.

"It is addressed to all three of us," Marcee said.

As the night grew colder and darker, the fire seemed brighter and more brilliant. The snow began to fall as a quiet peace settled over the three sisters. With the beautiful snow falling and covering the lawn, the night became bright. The lawn began to sparkle and shimmer with each snowflake that landed. Although it was getting colder, it didn't feel that way. The fire, now roaring, was so bright that it hid all of the shadows. They saw that it was a beautiful night.

In the fire's glow, Marcee placed the package on the hearth. As she began to remove the brown outer wrapping, a beautifully wrapped gift with a simple but eloquent bow and a tag was revealed. The tag read, "To Martha's three daughters."

Marcee quickly slid the bow from the present, keeping it intact. As she continued to peel back the wrapping, she was careful not to damage the contents. After having removed the paper, she lifted out a stark white box. As each piece of paper was removed, each sister began to feel a certain excitement anticipating what the box will hold. Slowly and cautiously, Marcee then lifted the lid from the box. Brilliant while tissue paper covered the unknown gift. Lifting each piece of tissue paper and casting it aside brought the sisters to a more peaceful feeling. Each layer removed felt like a part of their burden being cast aside. Less anxious then, by the third layer, they felt more hopeful and grateful and joyful. By the time they reached the last layer, before revealing the gift, they felt loved. Embracing their feelings, they relaxed. Surrounded with mounds of tissue paper, Marcee carefully lifted the gift.

In her hands was a small photo album. On the front of the album was a keyhole. A brass key was hanging from the strap holding the treasures inside. Marcee placed the key inside the golden lock and turned the key, unlocking her heart to accept the gift she was about to see. Opening the front cover, she read to her sisters the beautiful calligraphy inscription. It read, "This IS your Mother, Martha….She is Love, Laughter, Light, and Joy. We will miss her."

The words took root in the three sisters. They were foreign words written about a mother they thought they knew. Opposite the inscription was a photo of their mom clapping. She wore her oven mitts on her hands, her mouth was wide-open singing, and her eyes were filled with joy. They looked at each other and smiled remembering her happiness and joy while she sang at Lakeside. On the next page there were two more photos.

The first one was Martha wrapped in a big red boa covering a sparkling red gown, dancing with her hands in the air, a look of whimsy on her face. The inscription read "Oh how she loved to dance and act. What a clown!" Once again, they were struck with the oddness of the words describing their mother, but they all laughed again.

The third photo was Martha posing with her right hand on her right hip, a huge smile on her face. Her left hand was stretched forward as she displayed a huge costume-jeweled ring on her red painted finger. The treasure chest box sat on the table behind her. The look she wore said, *This is my special ring!* It might as well have been the Hope Diamond. The inscription read, "This is your mom's favorite. She proudly would say that her Bob gave it to her."

Turning the page again, there was one of Doris and Martha sitting together on the back patio, holding hands with a peaceful, content look on their faces. The sisters all sat quietly thinking of that special friend and the close relationship she shared with their mom.

The next page held a photo of Martha standing at an easel. She was concentrating intently on her painting. She had orange paint all over herself, the floor, the brush, and the paper. She looked ridiculous with her pressed lips and the intent look in her eyes, all the while wearing an orange blob of paint on her nose. The three women laughed hard then and talked of how much their mom enjoyed the painting days at Lakeside.

There were several more photos of them with Martha and one of her with Kathy. Martha had her arms around Kathy and they had aprons on. Their aprons were covered in flour, several shades of frosting, and sprinkles. They were standing in the kitchen. Martha was holding a cupcake with some sort of creature she had made on top of it, displaying it for the photographer to capture.

The very last picture was of Martha surrounded by her caregivers. They were wearing their green shrubs and the inscription read, "We all loved your mother, Martha. She has touched each of us in very special and unique ways. We were each blessed to have known her. You three sisters were blessed to have such a wonderful mother." Each of them had signed their names below their faces in the photograph.

Tears fill our eyes as we read their words. "Did we have a wonderful Mother?" were the thoughts streaming through each sister's mind, yet none of them would say it aloud. Yearning again for the joy felt in those few moments and not wanting the feeling of this special present to end,

Susan and Leslie continued to study the pictures in the album, and once again, their spirits were lifted and their mood lightened.

Sitting away from the others, Marcee sat quiet and still. She was thinking and pondering the question that still invaded her mind: "Were we blessed to have a wonderful Mother?"

Warmed now, her body started to tingle. She shivered and the hairs on the back of her neck stood on end. An unexpected feeling of love overwhelmed her and filled her with a presence so powerful that suddenly, she *knew*. In that moment God's spirit filled her, bringing with it His unending love. She was allowed a rare glimpse inside God's "why" world, the secret world of why things happen.

At that moment it suddenly became perfectly clear to her why their Dad had to go first, why they had to deal with two years of Alzheimer's disease with their mother, and why Martha had to lose her mind to that disease. God's plan was revealed to her in a brief moment in time. It was a revelation that took a moment of time for her to realize, but a lifetime to unfold. She knew then that this gift had to be shared, so she shared it with her sisters.

On that cold and sorrowful night, amidst their darkest hours, God was there with them. He had been there all the time. He had been there for eighty-two years. He was there revealing His gift of love to them all along, but especially during the last two years of their mom's life. He had a perfect plan, so brilliant and bright, that finally that night they were able to clearly see it.

MARCEE, SUSAN AND LESLIE: 2007

On July 14, 1925, God lovingly created our mother, Martha. As His child grew, those around her and the circumstances in her life influenced her self-perceptions. As she grew from a child to a young woman, a young woman to a wife, a wife to a mother, these outside influences molded her into the person she became and eventually into the mother we knew. She carried lots of baggage with her for most of her life, until the time she was blessed to get Alzheimer's disease.

In the end, she died not knowing her children, her grandchildren, or her husband. She did not even know herself. The person she had been most of her life was gone. Alzheimer's disease took it ALL away! The person she was created to be was left behind and her best parts remained; the raw, untainted, and unspoiled creature God had created eighty-two years before. The caregivers could see her clearly, and ultimately, she was there and visible for us, her daughters, to finally know and love.

That night, on the back patio of Marcee's house, our perceptions of our mother were changed and our brokenness healed. We think if Martha could have put it all into words herself, she might have said, "I got lost in the world and forgot who I was, but God didn't forget."

God created this little girl in His own likeness. He filled her with the gifts of kindness, humor, creativity, meekness and joy. He bestowed upon her passions of music and art. And He saw that she was good.

Epilogue

The aged, dark wooden floor squeaked as the mourners arrived. Dust floated delicately in the air as if under a microscope, magnified by the sunlight streaming through the windows that lined the small church. A feeling of warmth and peace filled the space. It had snowed that morning and the cool freshness of the air was a pleasant reminder that winter had arrived. A few family friends occupied the rows of benches in the old little church. It was a simple place, quite stark in appearance, but chosen for the simple truth of a life that had ended.

The sounds of hushed voices and soft piano music filled the air. Martha's family sat in the first several rows. The children wiggled as their parents tried desperately to keep them quiet and occupied.

Filling the other side of the first several rows sat mostly woman, clad in white and blue and green. Their laced shoes matched the cotton scrubs that they wore daily. Looking forward, all with the same gaze, they focused their attention towards the front of the church. Each wore a small and unique smile on their face as they sat thinking about the woman they had loved.

The only modern feature in the antique church was a simple spotlight embedded in the ceiling. It shone with a piercing brightness down upon an antique wooden pedestal. On the pedestal sat a gift. It was a beautifully wrapped present adorned with shiny silver paper. The beautiful package was tied with a large satin lace ribbon, painstakingly made with multiple loops of lace and ribbon. There was a white tag attached to the top. The light showered the gift with such a brilliant white that the gift glowed from its radiance.

Every eye was drawn to the simple gift that occupied the front of the church. The simple grandeur of the scene was mesmerizing. One couldn't help but be drawn to it. As the music ended, Martha's three daughters moved slowly but deliberately towards the front of the room. They stood together behind the pedestal. As the sisters look to the mourners before them, they saw faces intent on knowing what the gift before them held. Tears of joy and gratitude fill the sisters' eyes as they eagerly begin to share.

"Family and Friends," Susan began, "God has given us a gift." All eyes in the church move towards the pedestal.

"His gift to us is our mother," Leslie continued. All eyes moved from the gift on the pedestal to the three sisters.

Grabbing her sisters' hands, Marcee continued, "Today, we are honored to introduce you to our mother, Martha. We just met her for the first time, last night."

CPSIA information can be obtained at www.ICGtesting.com
Printed in the USA
LVOW12s2059310114

371843LV00002B/4/P